Onward Rising

Published March 2007, Fort Collins, CO, USA

Copyright 2007 Hauslendale Publishing

ISBN # 978-0-6151-5339-1

Disclaimer:

The story you are about to read is real, only the names have been changed to protect the innocent/guilty.

Table of Contents

This book is dedicated to the guides and the universe for leading me to my husband and for allowing us to create our own family together. I awake grateful and I go to bed grateful, thank you for such blessings.

Special thanks to all who have contributed to my life experiences that have allowed me to grow into what I am today and actually have the opportunity to write about it.

About the Author

Author Meilena Hauslendale began her career at a very young age working as a journalist, freelance and contributing author. In 1997, Meilena embarked on her career as an inspirational artist, initially developing her style by displaying her art along with inspirational sayings. Her work was then featured internationally through galleries and publications. It wasn't until 2002, that she began publishing her writing in the form of personal development articles and books.

She is the author of *Making Your Purpose, Your Business:* Guide to Self Discovery & Achievement, *Recognizing Unhealthy Relationships:* Guide to Healthy Love & Self Discovery, *Spiritual Revolution:* Guide to Spiritual Development & Independence, Natural Parenting: Guide to Pregnancy, Birth, & Beyond, and now Onward Rising – A Memoir.

The unique combination of art and literature had drawn recognition from both the art and writing community. In 2004, she was inducted into **Who's Who of American Women for 2004-2005,** the definitive biographical resource featuring the most accomplished women in all areas of human endeavor.

To read more about Meilena, please visit us at:

http://www.inspirationalauthor.com

and

http://www.meilena.com

Introduction

I began writing this book right before my 32nd birthday when I recently was put into contact with my biological father. The only way I knew how to brief him on my life up to this point was to write a book. I felt that I could document and somehow convey the journey given to me, the life led, and the life that is constantly at a state of becoming.

This is a story about a journey of intuitive guidance and dedication. It is through such shifts in our lives that we are directed towards our higher purpose. However, there are many steps we will need to take to go forward. Along our journey, we will encounter many obstacles that we will need to overcome to embrace our truth.

I used to always document my life by writing in journals ever since I was young. But with travels and moving frequently, it became more and more difficult to always port a box full of notebooks. So I found different ways to capture my life and moments through art, publishing articles, and books.

There was always so much I wanted to say to this man known as my father. There were so many moments both good and interesting that I wanted to share with him, but at the same time I was meant to journey alone. My being alone allowed me to develop an inner faith that could have never been taught to me by conventional means.

Intuitions are from an internally powered source. We often experience premonitions or visions that allow us to clarify our actions and decisions. I have expressed these intuitions throughout the book by placing them in *italics*. The occurrences are random however they are critical to my own personal development and are therefore displayed.

We each have a journey that we are to follow. We have a path set before us that branch off into several directions. We can take the hard earned lessons and neglect their teachings or we can choose to listen and learn, and use our experience to benefit the overall good of our society.

It is our decisions in this life that determine the outcome of not just ourselves, but those around us. We can choose to reciprocate negative behaviors and therefore contribute to negative outcomes. Or we can take a negative behavior or environment and use it to drive us to excel towards our highest being. We have the power to make this difference. We have the power to turn our life situations around and rise above them and move forward... move onward.

Chapter 1

the BEGINNING

I was born on April 17, 1975 in Tacoma Park, Maryland to a young married couple. My mother was 19 and my father was 18. Their relationship with one another was rather abrupt. Both were involved in drugs. Before my birth, my father went the extreme opposite and joined the Seventh Day Adventist Church and became a religious fanatic. He quit drugs and became a vegetarian. Then he spent hours daily devoted to the church.

His friends and loved ones would find him in meditation for long durations. Sometimes he would go to the highest point he could to be as close to God. He was once on top of a parking lot garage kneeling in a praying position right on the edge. Someone had called the police on him because they thought he was going to commit suicide. He was dragged off the edge still in a praying position from what was described to me by Judith.

He was known as a strange and unpredictable man. "But he was really good at playing guitar," my mother would say.

There were so many stories told, what was real and what was not, I never did know. It wasn't like I had the most reliable sources to ask either. I can assume. I can predict, but to those that lived and participated in my life, only bits and pieces were given to me about my father.

I guess my mother wanted to move back to Erie, PA to be with her family. Soon after we did, the relationship between the two had ended. As far as time frame, I guess I was one or two years old.

My mother came from a Catholic family of nine. There were seven girls and two boys born to my grandparents; my mother was the third child.

We had stayed with her parents for a while after she separated from my father. Living there was only a good excuse for my mother to leave me alone with her parents while she went out to party with her friends. I remember staring out the window overlooking the driveway, watching her effortlessly take off. My grandmother would tell me that she would be back soon. I looked at her and said, "No she won't."

I was right too. She would tell lies even then. She would tell her mother that she had to run out and get me a new bottle, but that wasn't the truth. Her behaviors were only setting the stage that lay ahead of us for many years to come.

At one point, she decided to pack up and move to Texas and live with an old girlfriend for a while. So we hopped on a greyhound and travelled there. Not having anyone around to "contain" her, gave my mother all the more reason to be irresponsible. She did a lot of drinking and drugs while she was there.

I remember wandering out on the balcony on top of the high rise apartments where we stayed at. I shut the sliding door and locked myself out. I was banging on the sliding door for someone to come get me and it felt like it took forever.

At one point she was so drunk while she was there, she had invited people back to her friend's apartment and then passed out drunk. The people she brought over robbed her friend's apartment while she was passed out. Her friend kicked us out after that. We had no money to fall back on either. During that time, my mother always told me she stole food for me at the convenience stores so I could eat.

She called a male friend of hers from back home named Isaac, and told him what was going on. She didn't even have money for us to get back to Erie. So the guy felt bad for her and sent her the money for the tickets to go back.

We moved back in with my grandparents and Judith started dating Isaac. Isaac partied too, but he was a laid back guy. You would look at him and think he was a big teddy-bear-looking biker. He was from the neighborhood there in Erie. He grew up only blocks away from Judith's parent's house on June Street. Judith actually went to high school with Isaac at East High. He was even friends with my biological father, Patrick.

I always was so grateful for Isaac helping us and giving us the money to get back to Erie. I think I even knew then that Judith was not that stable of a parent. I looked after her. I worried about her. I was this little girl worrying about my mom constantly.

Judith knew a lot of people, but that's because of her drug habit. I remember going to different drug dealers houses when I was little. The same thing always happened. The woman or guy would get their "special" box out and then take their Zig Zag paper card and scrape out a stash for my mom, shove it in a ziplock bag, and then weigh it on a scale. The deal would be closed with the smoking of a joint.

There I was in innocence watching it all, breathing the same air they were. We didn't have much money, but she had pot. We didn't have much money, but she had alcohol, and she had cigarettes. We were already on welfare and assistance, but what money we had was spent on these things.

I tagged along with her to the bars. She would get me a bag of chips and a soda and let me sit up on a barstool to play a pinball game at the Shaggy Dog. Then she would meet up with someone that would offer to get her high and off we would go.

Before they put the Bayfront Highway in down by the Public Dock, which is now known as Dobbins Landing, there was a huge overlook across from Hamot Hospital. The brick road is still there today, but the cliff is not so steep and now there is a safety fence.

The idiot she left the bar with drives us over on this cliff. I sit in the back just dangling around this large boat of a car. They have the windows rolled all the way up while they sit there smoking a few bowls together. The man says, "What would you do if I just drove us over this cliff right now?" And then he starts easing the car forward. Mind you the guy is blitzed now and can hardly keep his eyes open. My mom is laughing and I'm in the back seat with a sober look on my face. The more he hears me protest, the more he eases the car forward. Finally, we leave and make it back to the 10-speed bike with my kidseat on the back at the bar. I would have rather sat and played pinball.

In between erratic behaviors, we would go to parks and feed birds. That was my most favorite time of all. We would feed the little pigeons down on Perry Square, after we got fresh roasted peanuts from Greg's Place up the street. I would play in the fountain. It was those little things that I loved. It was those little times when my mom decided to be a mom that meant the most to me. Unfortunately, those moments began to come few and far between as her alcoholism and addictions progressed.

Judith was no dummy, but she knew how to play dumb quite frequently. If she lived on her own, she could do what she wanted, drink when she wanted, smoke pot when she wanted. If she lived at home with her parents, the only thing she could sneak by was drinking. She couldn't smoke her cigarettes or pot in the house.

So we managed somehow to live in a few apartments close to the downtown. She had friends she would invite over here and there. I think that was the most responsible time I can think of in her life because nobody else was there to pick up any slack. Nobody else was there to enable her unhealthy behaviors.

Judith would see Isaac on and off. Judith had a history with Isaac. She was always a sporadic woman and Isaac was a more traditional man on the outside. He became a journeyman and an electrician. He got a local job there in Erie at an old machine shop called RD&D. So his footing there was secured. Judith looked towards Isaac as a stable man that cared a lot for her.

Isaac was the ideal caretaker. He was a passive man. Judith on the other hand was the aggressor. He was calm and Judith was the go-getter, but she never knew what to focus her drive on. She liked to sing and play guitar and was actually quite good at it, but she was easily swayed and would lose focus too quickly.

We eventually moved in with Isaac in several apartments and then the two of them were married at a local Justice of the Peace, right by the Country Fair convenience store. They were married in Harley t-shirts and leathers.

She then wanted me to start calling this person "Dad." I was a little stubborn at first with this. I knew I had a real father even then, but I was told over and over how crazy and mental he was. It crushed me and nobody knew. Nobody wanted to know. After all, I was a kid.

I had dreams of my real father though and I knew what he looked like. I watched him very carefully even if it was only spiritually.

One night in my dream, I saw Patrick at the Arts Festival downtown walking alone. I told my mom that I saw him down at Perry Square at the Arts Festival. She just shrugged me off and told me, "oh, that's nice."

Months later we went to Newt's campground out in Waterford, PA and a mutual acquaintance of Patrick and Judith was there. He said, "Hey Judith, I saw Patrick a little while ago at the Arts Festival." I spoke up immediately and described to the man what I saw Patrick wearing in my dream. He looked at me and said, "How did you know that, were you there?"

I just looked at my mom and just said, "I saw him in my dream." And I walked off. They were all sitting around the picnic table drinking and smoking their bowls of pot. Judith quickly changed the subject, but I heard the guy say to her later on, "Judith, how did she know that?"

Despite all that was conveyed to me about my father, I still felt I had an attachment to him, even at that young of an age. I just couldn't explain it yet, nor was there any one that I could justly confide in either.

It was just something I had to pacify myself with for a long time. I still had his last name though. Even though my mom was married to Isaac, my last name from Patrick was still there. So I had "something" and I was proud of that.

For others it was only a reminder of someone they didn't really care too much about.

I soon began conforming to my mother's wishes and called Isaac "Dad." He was the only male role model present in my life. I was grateful for him. He put food on the table and he made sure there was a roof over our heads, both for me and my mom. Once they were married, Judith soon realized she could do just about anything she wanted and get away with it all.

If Isaac was working then Judith didn't have to always keep a job. So she worked at different places here and there, but her income would just compensate for what she spent on alcohol and drugs.

While Isaac and Judith went out and partied, I would be left with babysitters that would wind up locking me in my bedroom so they could make-out with their boyfriends. If I was lucky my grandparents would watch me. They had a big house right on June Street where my mom grew up. I always thought I felt safe there until one of the times I was left there overnight. One night, one of my mom's sisters, Lynn, began sexually confronting and touching me.

The next day, I told my mom when she came back home, right in front of Lynn and the rest of the family. My mom never believed me and then she told me that it was normal for family to "experiment" with one another. I stopped associating myself with Lynn. I told several people in the family and everyone just covered it up. Nobody would speak up about it, not even my own mother. In fact, she still had me sleep over there.

I made sure that I never slept in the same bed with her sister again. I stayed as far away from her as I could. Even if I had to be in the same house with her, I made sure I was distant.

I started to sleep in the same bed with my other Aunt Peggy. My grandparent's house was so huge to me. It was three stories high, but you had to share a bed with someone because of all the people living there. Plus I was little so I felt secure to sleep with someone.

That night my Aunt Peggy would ask me for a kiss goodnight. I gave her a kiss, just a peck on the lips, like any kid would do. She told me, that's not a real kiss. I didn't know what she meant. Then she said, "This is a real kiss," and stuck her tongue in my mouth.

I never said anything to anyone after feeling foolish for doing so with Lynn. I kept my mouth shut, but soon made sure I slept by myself.

Soon after, an opportunity opened up for us to have our own house, right up the street from my grandparent's house on June Street. Isaac's grandmother lived on the corner of June and Linwood. One of the house's she owned right beside of her was vacant. So she let us rent it out. We moved into that house when I was about 4 years old. This would be the place where I would live until I was 17, this would be the final dance hall.

Chapter 2

the Final Dancehall

I can still remember the first night we spent together in the little white house on 2312 June Street. The floors were bare and the burnt sienna carpet wasn't laid out just yet. We didn't have beds, so we made a pallet on the floor in the living room and slept there.

My room would be the little room beside the master bedroom which wasn't the nicest of rooms. You could barely fit a crib in there. The walls were thin in that house no matter where you were, so any sexual drunken fury could be heard whether you were upstairs or downstairs, but it was home... my home.

I started going to preschool about a block away when my mom started working at one of the packing facilities there. I would get up at about six in the morning and be taken off to preschool. Preschool was fun for me. I got to be around other kids for a change. Being the only child, I often longed for a playmate. My mother had her tubes tied after she gave birth to me so there was no chance of me having a sibling.

Preschool also set me up for Judith demonstrating her lack of dependability. There were times where she would be very late picking me up due to drugs or drinking. I would be so sad when that happened. I would watch all the kids being picked up by their sober parents and then nothing. The cars cleared out. The children cleared out and the only two people left were me and my preschool teacher. I was so embarrassed even then. This would not be the first time she would do this either. I would just burst into tears when she wouldn't show up.

Isaac began working even more. He was still at the same place, but would work long hours, come home, eat, and then pass out on the couch. He was always very quiet. He would be passed out sleeping and Judith would be out with her friends partying. That was the typical week night. When she started dealing dope out of the house, she would stay at home and drink, but that meant we had more odd people coming through the house.

Isaac and Judith relationship was one out of convenience. He provided this sense of stability, so that Judith felt comfortable enough to be irresponsible and reckless. Their relationship was based on sexual dependency and not based on love. If they weren't having sex then they were arguing.

Isaac hated arguing and Judith loved it. She was the antagonist. She knew what buttons to push and when to push them. She knew just what to say to make someone feel like shit. Perhaps it was her own guilt and self hatred that made her lash out on people, but whatever it was, she just loved drama. If there wasn't drama around someone else, she would create drama around herself.

Isaac was a great guy. He took care of Judith, looked after her, but he also covered up for her, and enabled her to stay sick. You never knew what she was going to get into, where she would be that night, and if she would even come home alive. She was always out driving around drunk and blacking out. As for the morning-afters, I was her caretaker. I would take her boots off when she came home. I would give her 7up when she was hung-over. I would put her cigarettes out for her when she would pass out with them still lit. I was her mother, always wondering why she would do this to herself.

I stared at a woman gone bad, as she laid there in bed, her skin bruised from falling around while intoxicated. Oh the smell that came from her skin, how foul it was. Just a woman filled of alcohol along with an ash tray full of cigarette buds and the sour stench of drunken sex permeated the room.

They were so oblivious to what I was witnessing, both of them. By the time I was five, I started attending Diehl School which was also a block away. I started kindergarten now which meant going to school for half days. Judith would forget to pick me up on several occasions and be late. Eventually I was just given a house key and taught how to walk home which saved me from the embarrassment and disappointment.

When I started kindergarten, I also had times when I would peer through people. I could see auras around all the children, although I didn't know what auras were yet. It was their energy that I could see form a ring around them. I think I told my mother about what I could see and she made me go get my eyes checked.

I don't think she could see people's auras. If she saw anything out of focus it was because she was too drunk to see straight, not because she was picking up or sensing someone's energy field. I would try to shake these visions I saw as I didn't know that it was ok to see them, but no matter what I did the auras were there. I could stare at the kids going down the hall and watch their energy bounce off and collide into one another. While they were screaming and amusing themselves, I was quietly staring at them.

I soon found out that my life was not like everyone else's life, especially when it came down to family. I remember distinctly sitting in our little chairs gathering around the table in kindergarten and our teacher doing flash cards with us. She placed one card up that showed a cooking pan, but the word below said "P-O-T." The teacher said to the class this is a "pot."

I spoke up before the whole class and said innocently, "that's not pot, pot is what my Mom and Dad smoke." The teacher looked so embarrassed and my class looked very puzzled. The teacher spoke to me after class. She told me about a program called TIP (Turn In a Parent). So I went home and told Judith the next time she went to go roll her joints up, that what she was doing was wrong and that I could turn her in for it.

She was so pissed off at me. So now she was like a little kid having to go outside to smoke her dope. She would try hiding her pipe under the picnic table too if I came out. Her hiding her habit didn't last long though. She got over our talk, and started doing it right in front of me again. Only now she would tell me that I shouldn't tell others about this.

I looked at all the kids around and noticed how different we were all being kept. If you ever feel bad about your life, know that somewhere, someone always has it worse than you. No matter what happened to me emotionally, I kept that state of mind present, that there was always someone out there having to endure something worse.

I think the sad thing was I didn't realize the mess I was in. I was sitting in a pile of dirt and somewhere, somebody told me it was "clean," but they were wrong. Judith was the only mother I ever had and Isaac was the only form of a father I ever had, who was I to know there was a difference between functional parents and dysfunctional parents?

I had suspicions, but I didn't know. If I knew, I didn't want to. Sometimes it is easier living with madness if you don't admit it is there. I adapted. I tolerated unacceptable behavior. This was my life and I knew nothing different. What was crazy is that every one around me was just standing by watching and then covering up or shrugging off any irrational actions. There were things that didn't seem to be "right," but yet here were all these adults in Judith's family that were indicating to me that it was "no big deal." So they had taught me to do the same.

Every time Judith drank she would tag me along with her. She would always drink and drive with me in the car. I would have to tell her she was going over the line on the road. I would have to tell her to watch out for the car. Somehow we would make it home unharmed. I would pray that we made it home okay and we did. I was too little to drive. All I could do is somehow be her "eyes," and be the one with the sober perspective. I hoped and I prayed for us always.

On the nights that she drank out with her friends from work, she drove home drunk by herself. I would always go check the car to see the scratches on the side, to see if she hit anyone. There would be different colors left behind from each different car that she hit.

One night we even had the cops come to our doorstep. I answered the door and then they would ask for my mom or dad.

Isaac quickly came to the door. He was probably afraid of what I would have said. Here the whole street by our house reported a hit and run of parked cars the night before. Isaac told the cops some story that his wife was taking medication that made her sleepy and she may have hit them coming home from work and not realized it.

Isaac could tell a story and you would believe him in a heartbeat. He seemed like an honest man and you would look at him and think he could do no wrong. So the cop believed him and that was it. She never was taken away or charged for anything.

Not all nights were like that though. I do remember another time that the cops came to the door and issued a warrant for my mother's arrest. And then she had to explain to me that she had to go to jail for something she did. She told me some story, but it was obvious some trouble went on. She had bruises all over her, a gash above her eyebrow. She was drunk again, so there was no telling what had happened.

She could tell you anything and you had no way of knowing if it was the truth or not. You always wanted to believe that the person you care about does no wrong. You want to believe they are in the right, but that's not always the case.

While my every day life with Judith's addictions continued, I was trained by Isaac not to tell anyone about what went on. He was the primary enabler, the one that wanted everything to look "perfect," but we were so far from that. I wanted to be so honest and I was. I would get in trouble for that too.

If her family called, I would have to say she is sick and not feeling well, but I would always blurt out, "she is hung-over." Then Isaac would rush to get on the phone and say, "yeah she came down with the stomach flu." Trying to hide Judith's alcoholism was like trying to hide an elephant in the living room. No matter what you do, that elephant is still there.

My intuitions and premonitions kept me alive. One night I was supposed to go out with Judith and Isaac out to Edinboro to go fishing with them and their two friends. I always loved getting out of the house, but for some reason, my gut was telling me not to go. I told Judith that I wanted to spend the night over my grandparent's house instead.

I remember Judith asking me if I was sure I didn't want to go, she said, "Are you sure, you always like going with us?" I assured though that I was going to stay with my grandparents.

That night the phone rang at my grandparent's house. I listened intently. I was upstairs so I had no way of knowing what was going on, but when my grandma called up the stairs, I told her, "They got in an accident and were at the hospital. They are okay though." I caught my grandma off guard, she said, "But how did you know?" I said, "I just knew."

If I would have been with them that night, I probably would have been flown through the windshield because we didn't have seatbelts in the back seat and there were no laws enforcing them yet. The truck they were driving had bucket seats and I always sat in the center of the back seat and sometimes even in the front on the compartment. They were hit by a drunk driver head on. The drunk driver died on contact.

Amongst all our daily and weekly dramas at home, I was in school. I loved school because when I was at school, I was not at home. When I was at school, I was not left alone all the time. I got to actually do things with others. I got to learn. I focused my energy on learning. I focused my sadness on learning.

Learning was all I had to look forward to. I would be studying at home amongst fighting and arguments. It helped me deal with the turmoil. I would read books all the time. I would put little charts up in my bedroom and set goals for myself.

Thinking back to that time, I even realized then in an indirect way, that I couldn't change other people, I could only change myself. So I did everything I could to be a better "me." I read, I got involved in music. I would even stay after school to help the teachers' correct homework in first and second grade.

My parents and family life was a mystery to people at school. Nobody saw my family unless it was by some accident and then they would always be shocked. Judith came to a school outing to the zoo one time and it was so embarrassing because she was hungover and just reeked of alcohol. One of the little girl's mothers even said to her, "do you realize you smell like alcohol?"

That was the first and the only school event she went to. Even on my little birthday parties, she would wind up drinking during them and then get drunk. Doing normal things just became more of an embarrassment than a joy. You couldn't enjoy your birthday because you were worried about your mom getting so drunk she would lose her bladder and other people would see.

So slowly but surely, birthday parties would just consist of her friends and maybe my grandma or a few of her sisters. Any excuse she had to drink, she would drink. That was all there was to it. At most she could drink a night was about a case of beer to herself. Our refrigerator was always stocked with beer. Didn't have a whole lot of food in the refrigerator but we had beer.

Now don't get me wrong, I never went hungry. Judith and Isaac were both heavier weighing individuals, so food was always around, but the types of food we had was another story. That was one of the things the two of them could do besides for argue or have sex and that was eat.

Isaac was different with drinking, he had a shut off valve and Judith did not. He couldn't keep up with her when it came to drinking. He always had a cut off point when he had enough. This was good for me if we were out somewhere together because Isaac would at least be able to drive us home. I dreaded any events that involved drinking simply because I knew what the outcome would be. I knew my mom would be drunk and would not want to leave. I knew she would be obnoxious. I knew that she would be loud. I knew she would try to argue with Isaac.

Unfortunately, the only outings we would go to involved drinking. Shop picnics, fishing, family functions, dinners, all would involve drinking. Isaac and I would desperately try to contain the monster too, but she was *on* the moment she had access to any alcohol. She would get high before she went into a social function to help her nerves around a lot of people and then the drinking would commence.

My mom always worked jobs that supported her behaviors too. Like I said, the woman was no dummy, she could manipulate and twist anyone in to believing she was telling the truth and doing the right thing. I think in some aspects she thrived on that.

She worked your average production line job, where all you had to do is show up and work the line. Granted these jobs are repetitive and demanding because you are on your feet all day, but they are also the perfect job for alcoholics. She could also do the job while she was stoned which was the added bonus.

Other people she worked with were partiers too so she fit right in. Her environment was the perfect place for an alcoholic to thrive because nobody would complain about what you are doing if they are doing it themselves. If your boss is out there getting stoned with you in the parking lot before work, they are not going to turn you in for showing up hung-over or strung out. So this certainly worked well for her for several years.

She had everything an alcoholic needed to thrive on; a husband that paid the bills, a husband that would be there at night to be with her kid, someone that would lie for her, and a paycheck to support her habit. It was a recipe for disaster.

Where was I through all of this? I was where a daughter thought she should be, right by her mother's side. That is, when she was there. I went home to an empty house a lot. Isaac worked late all the time and Judith worked late too so I would get off from school and come home to an empty house. I had a key to the front door so that I could let myself in. This was pretty much the way of life while I was in elementary school.

I started getting into playing the cello during this time too and would lug a huge cello home from the school so that I could practice. I would carry that big heavy thing a whole block. It seemed like it took forever to get home especially with a backpack full of books.

One night we got a call about Isaac's grandmother. I had answered the phone and then handed the phone to Isaac. I didn't know why they were calling yet, but I told Isaac his grandmother had passed away and they must be calling to tell us. I was right. The next few nights I would have visions of her. She was no longer restricted by her physical body. We played cards and she talked to me about where she was going. We never really spoke before even when we visited her, but now she was talking to me. I can't remember what she had said to me, but after the funeral, I never heard from her again.

My bedroom eventually migrated upstairs to the cold attic. The house was never insulated well and had a draft even on normal days. This bedroom gave me the space I needed to retreat to, when I didn't want to be in the middle of any arguments between Isaac and Judith.

I could do whatever I wanted up there. I would study, practice my cello, and sing. I could also write in privacy which was the greatest thing to me. Judith always thought I was weird for wanting to retreat and write. But for me it was just a way to deal with everything in a quiet way. I could never write about what was truly going on though. I had to write in a way that was cryptic to her because she would sneak upstairs and rummage through my writings, just trying to find something to get on to me about.

If I was ever to complain about anything remotely, she would scream and yell at me telling me, "You know how good you have it..." So in a weird way, I thought maybe I had it good. Maybe I was fortunate. Well yes I was fortunate, fortunate to develop a good head on my shoulders despite chaos.

Kids misbehave and I was no different. There were times that I would get on my mother's nerves a little more than she would like, but I never did anything out of the ordinary of 6-8 year old kid. On several occasions she threatened to take me to a girl's home, "A home for bad girls," she would say. She would even go as far as putting me in the car and driving me to the girl's home out in Harborcreek. She would pull right there in the parking lot. She would do this without Isaac knowing or anyone from her family for that matter. Then she would go on this dramatic escapade with me and make me beg her to not give me away.

And sure that threat scared me. I already lost one part of me, my father. I didn't want to lose the other part of my family, no matter how deranged it was.

So I always tried to be on best behavior and be a good daughter.

During all of these years, I would get severe headaches that would make me sick for days. My mother would take me to the doctor and they would check me out and never could pinpoint why this would happen. I know now that it was a result from the intense stress of my environment.

Judith thrived on medical conditions. I over heard her talking to a family member on the phone while I was upstairs, "We just have to take it day by day. She may have brain cancer you know..." I remember thinking to myself where was I when they told her this? What is she even talking about? Whatever she could do to get a reaction out of someone, she would do it.

When you are constantly up against a stressful home life and you are not even fully aware of the magnitude, your body eventually shuts itself down. Even as a child I was nervous. I never knew what would await me when I came home. It was almost a relief if nobody was there. I could come home and breathe for a moment and prepare myself mentally for what would happen at night.

Isaac coped with it by not talking. He would go to work, come home, eat, take a nap, call the bars to find out where Judith was at that night, and maybe try to go pick her up. I would be left alone.

I didn't have parents that would sit down and read to me. I didn't have parents that would help me do my homework, but that never stopped me from trying. One time, I made the mistake of encouraging my mom to participate in helping me with my homework. Oh how I thought that moment was great! I turned my homework in the next day and failed each answer. I never asked her to help me again.

There was too much going on with both Isaac and Judith that there was no time for much of anything else. She had her pattern and Isaac had his role. No matter what he did, the results were always the same. If she was mad, she would drink, if she was happy, she would drink. It didn't matter at all. If there was an excuse to drink, she would find it.

Chapter 3

the Adoption

I was in the 4th grade when my mother told me that I had to have my last name changed from my biological father's last name to Isaac's last name. I was very devastated with this request, but couldn't oppose it. My mother explained to me that I had to do this to get on Isaac's health insurance and so he can claim me on his taxes. Perhaps she didn't anticipate me asking why I needed my last name changed and just came up with this explanation, I never knew fully.

She explained to me that we would need to go to court and that there was a chance that Patrick, my biological father, might show up to protest the change. I secretly hoped he would. I secretly wished with excitement that I would finally be able to meet this man once and for all and that I wouldn't have to have my name changed. My last name was the one tie that I had left of my father. I held onto that dearly for many years and now it was soon to be taken away from me.

As far as I knew Patrick was in and out of mental facilities though. I was told that he did drugs and went insane. Perhaps this was true, but I still had respected the man enough to want to know of him. After all, I loved Judith and she was insane by choice.

So they proceeded with the name change and a month or so later I was dressing up to go to court. Judith kept telling me, "Now Patrick might be there to protest this." I was scared and I was nervous all at the same time.

The reality of this unknown to me at the time was that Patrick probably didn't even know about my adoption proceeding. And if he did find out, it would be after the fact when the name was already changed.

As far as I knew, he was battling his mental illness all these years and never had any contact with me or my mother. I was told he never paid child support and never made any attempts to see me whatsoever. I didn't even know if he comprehended having a daughter, but that never would stop me of thinking of him.

I would try finding out whatever I could from anyone that I could. I would ask my grandparents or my aunts. I wanted answers. Everything I heard was so elusive. They all told me recycled stories that Judith had told them.

Judith always told me that Patrick was weird. He thought that my mother and I were the devil trying to keep him away from God. She told me that he wouldn't give me my bottle one time when I was hungry because he needed to "break me of my will." She told me that one night she found him painting the Ten Commandments on my bedroom wall while I was sleeping, with a machete underneath my crib.

These are the things that I was told, but to me there had to be more. I just couldn't put my finger on what "more" there was and if I would ever have the glory of finding out the truth no matter how bitter sweet it may be. Would he know me? Would he know my face? Would he wonder what I was becoming?

The reality of my name change sunk in when I went to school and wrote on my paper the name I was accustomed to, and the teacher told me I could no longer use that last name as that would be illegal, that I had to use my new last name from now on. I think I stared at her blankly for a moment and then reluctantly wrote my new last name.

In some ways though, I felt bad for Isaac. He never had children of his own and I was the closest thing to a child that he had, so I wanted to some how honor him for allowing me to be his daughter. I viewed taking his last name as a form of my gratitude. There was no telling where my mom and I would have been, had he not been in our lives to provide some form of stability.

Patrick never did show up at the court proceedings so Judith didn't have that fuel to embellish with her drinking companions. A new drama soon took its place in the ring.

I was in 5th grade by this time. I enjoyed singing in the school choir and playing my cello at our little school recitals. I even talked my mom into going to one of them. I believe she also was encouraged by a neighbor, one of her best of friends, who was attending because her daughter was in the recital as well.

I always did very well in school. I had excellent grades and was able to pick things up very quickly. I loved conquering a challenge and learning was certainly one of those challenges. I liked having goals to focus on. It helped me not focus so much on what was going on around me and it gave me something to look forward to.

When October rolled around while I was in 5th grade, my mom promised me she would take me to the store and buy me some curtains for my room. I never had nice curtains in my bedroom, just two cheap valances she bought years ago that were just riddled in dust. So after many years with these top covers I asked for some curtains. I was always afraid to ask for anything because of money being so tight, but I some how got the courage to ask for this.

I was so excited, my mom actually agreed to take me to Value City to pick out curtains. She said she would pick me up after school that day and we could go pick them out. I could hardly sleep that night. I was so excited. The next day she came and picked me up from school late, but I was still keeping my enthusiasm about the whole ordeal, giving her the benefit of the doubt. Maybe something came up and that was why she was late.

I flew open the school doors to the parking lot and there she was, the only car there, a huge old maroon boat that Isaac and I called the "bash mobile." It was an old Chrysler, pure steel; the bumpers were bashed and slightly dented. It was not like the compact automobiles that we have today. This car was a tank. Thank God for that car too, because it was the armor that kept this woman safe from her own mishaps.

When I saw her from a distance waiting for me in the parking lot, I knew something was wrong. You could feel her energy before you even approached the car.

I got into the car and she looked at me and said, "I have to tell you something." I was worried because she was crying and hysterical. I said, "Mom what is wrong, is everything ok?" She said, "I have to tell you something, you have a half-brother." Then she proceeds to tell me that today was the birthday of her first child that she had when she was 16. Her parents forced her to give the child up for adoption to the Catholic Child Services.

She was terribly drunk when she told me this in the car. After she confessed to me in the parking lot, we drove off. She pulled into the driveway of my grandparent's house, only blocks away, and tells me to go over there for a while. She asks me to not say anything about this to her Mom, so I agree. I open the door to my grandparent's house and there was my grandma.

I was just told not to say anything, so I respected my mother and didn't tell my grandma what she just told me, or that she was drunk for that matter. My grandma was like, "Isn't she going to come in or anything?" But my mom had already peeled out of the driveway and was gone. I never did get curtains and I never would.

Someone eventually bought me a mini blind for the small window that faced the neighbor's house, but that wasn't until my teenage years. Up till that point anyone could see in my room.

After 5th grade, I would transition into middle school which meant I had to start taking the bus. Boy did everything change. All of a sudden popularity became a huge factor and the kids around me got a lot meaner. Sixth grade was hard. I was a good student and now started to get picked on for it. Not to mention my clothes were scraggly hand-me-downs from my aunts. They weren't too bad of clothes, but they didn't fit me very well. I would only get a couple of new outfits before school started and a few more at Christmas.

My hair was long and uncut. I kept it back in a headband which wasn't suitable for my face and I wore glasses. The doctor and my mother insisted I needed glasses for many years, but they gave me terrible headaches. It wasn't until I moved to California as an adult that I had them rechecked and was told I didn't even need to wear glasses.

But nonetheless, I respected my mom. She told me to wear the glasses, so I wore the glasses. My weight wasn't the greatest either. I was 116 pounds in the 6th grade. I had obese parents as my eating role models. I was teased about my weight a lot by the other kids. My girlfriend Jen that I would walk to the bus stop with would befriend me as soon as we got around others. It was a big slap in my face. Again, I could trust no one.

Nobody had any idea what was going on in my life. I still kept myself active in school. I joined the newspaper club so I could write. I did everything that I could to keep myself motivated. I wanted to succeed more than anything. I was just determined to not be like my family.

That year was certainly a transitional year, not to mention I went to a lower Eastside public school that had a lot of hard edged kids. There were probably others that had the same type of life, but they used it to roughen themselves up. They would go around starting fights all the time. They were already smoking, having sex, making out in the parking lot, and skipping school. Their parents didn't give a shit and either did they.

The bus rides home were the worst. I would be ganged up on and picked on by the group. My girlfriend Jen would act like she didn't know me until we would get off the bus. She became my friend real quick one day when we were being chased by two boys after we got off the bus. They chased us and pelted us with pieces of the blacktop from the street. Jen got hit in the head and was crying. I had her run with me down to my grandma's house so they wouldn't see where we both lived, and finally they stopped chasing us.

I didn't get to go out a lot, but my Aunt Jeanie, who I respected the most out of all Judith's sisters, would take time to take me places. She would take me for bike rides and take me on the bus to take the fairy over to the beach. She would take me shopping with her. And she was sober the whole time which was a new way of watching someone.

She gave me one-on-one time. She didn't have to have a ton of people around her to be with me. I always admired her so much for going against everyone and dedicating time to me.

She eventually went off to a state college which was only 45 minutes outside of Erie, but it meant that I saw her less and less, because she lived on campus. So from 3rd grade to about 7th grade she would be in college for nursing school.

That summer Isaac bought me the greatest gift ever. It was a book subscription called "Just For Girls." I would get a book every month. The first book was about how to take care of yourself. That was something certainly new to me. I was so focused on my mother being happy, being alive, or Isaac being happy, that I wasn't taking good care of myself, and I didn't know how to either.

I knew how to take care of someone when they were sick. I knew how to do my laundry. I knew how to wash the dishes and vacuum, but I didn't know how to take care of myself in a personal way. So I read my book. It would tell me how much I should weigh in range of my height. I found out I was about 16 pounds overweight, so I started to watch what I ate, but secretly.

That summer I lost 16 pounds and could actually fit into girls sizes instead of junior women. I wanted to change my hair too. I always had it long. I always had psoriasis too which was a crust that forms on your scalp. We never knew what it was caused by, but later on in life, I found out that it is triggered by excessive stress.

I got my first perm which was awful looking. Somehow these ladies chopped off my hair and gave me the tightest perm known to man which was crazy. I started to read about doing your hair. I learned how to curl my hair. I practiced it like anything else in my life, until I got good at it.

By the time eighth grade began, I showed up at school and nobody recognized me. I had completely transformed myself. The teacher would call out my name and I would answer, and everyone would be shocked at what I looked like. I made some very big changes.

I was 13 now. People at school started to notice me, boys started to notice me. They began to be curious about who I was. By that time I had just had enough with people and their crap. I wasn't going to allow people to walk over me anymore. I wasn't going to allow people to hit me or tease me. I started fighting back. I had a boy start a confrontation with me in the hallway. I spoke up for myself, and then he started choking me, so I fought back. I had this fuel that was building up in me and I wasn't going to take anything from anyone... anymore. We both were put in ISS (In School Suspension). Didn't matter who started it either, we both had the same penalty.

It was the first time I got into any trouble like that. Judith hid this from Isaac for some reason. I was so upset and disappointed in myself for the suspension that I was very honest with Judith about what went on. She told me, "We're not going to tell your Dad about this." I didn't ask questions about her reasoning either.

Meanwhile at home, I had to contend with a suicidal mother. She would sit there at the dinner table right in front of me with a huge knife telling me she was going to kill herself, telling me what kind of tombstone she wanted. She would on several occasions even say, "Let's go for a ride," and then take me to a tombstone maker facility and tell me what kind of tombstone she wanted when she dies. She wanted drama. She wanted you to react whether it was tears or not. She got off on your reaction.

Her sporadic behavior always kept you guessing. You never knew what each day was going to bring. One day I woke up for school and went downstairs to go to the bathroom. I pulled my pants down and go to sit on the toilet seat and almost sit on mother! She had passed out on the toilet. Scared me to death. I had to wake her up and send her to bed.

Another time, I would be headed out the door to catch my bus for school, and here Judith would be passed out in the front yard. I would check to see if she was alive, and then wake her up, and get her in the house.

I mentioned that we lived up the street from her parents. Well right beside their house was a bar on the corner of Buffalo Road and June Street called Bogey's Tavern. That's where she would go have drinks at, but then she would get so drunk, she couldn't walk back home. So she would literally crawl up the street.

Funny thing was her parents always listened to the police scanner they had, and sat out on the front porch in the dark, late at night. So they watched their daughter Judith crawl up the street to our house.

She was drinking more than ever and started getting into more drugs. She would be gone for days at a time now on drug binges. Isaac called me home from a friend's house one time and said I had to come home right away, that he would be there to pick me up. I had no idea what was going on. I just knew it had something to do with my mother. He drove up to my friend's house and I hopped into the car. He said, "Your mom is living in a trailer with some lady she started doing coke with. She won't come home for me so I told her you were really sick and she needed to come home right away." So he told me I had to be home when she called so I could go along with his lie. She eventually called and Isaac convinced her to come home.

Chapter 4

breaking The Girl

I called her "Judith" for a long time. I wouldn't even call her a mother. I told her once she started to act like a mother, I would call her one, but for now she was Judith. One night, I had enough. I couldn't put up with her any longer. I got down on my knees and I cried and I prayed so hard. I wrote on my floor to God, "I GIVE UP." I told God that I couldn't take care of this woman any longer. I don't know how long I sat and prayed. That very next morning, Isaac called up the stairs to my room and told me, we got your mom into rehab this morning. I called to God quietly and said, "thank you."

You better believe I prayed every day and said "thank you." No matter what my day was like, I made sure to say those words, because every day had a lesson. Every day taught me something whether I wanted it to or not.

"She had to take a few wine coolers with her on the way, but they got her admitted," Isaac said. If people thought I was alone before, I was really alone now. Both Isaac and Judith were emerged in meetings now. Isaac went to Al-Anon and Judith joined Alcoholics Anonymous. It was the best thing for her. She was in rehab for 30 days at which time her family got involved and helped us paint the inside of our house, and put a new kitchen floor in to replace the torn up linoleum that was gaping with dirt.

I helped out as much as I could. Again everyone would just go out of their way to make her feel happy so that she wouldn't have to complain so much about her life. When Judith drank she blamed everyone but herself. Everyone else had the problem. Everyone else was the reason why she drank.

When she began her journey on getting sober, the affects of her drinking habit took a toll on her body.

Her liver had slight damage from the abuse and her DTs (Delirium tremens) were very heavy. She had the shakes for about 2 years after getting sober. Her head would just bob back and fourth.

I would go to visit her in rehab at Serenity and I would go to meetings with her. I supported her on her path to sobriety. I still didn't trust her and I had to keep my distance from her emotionally, for my own protection and stability, but I supported her. Every Friday, I would go to the midnight meeting with her down at the Al-canon Club.

I soon began my own negative behavior and experimentation. I started smoking cigarettes. I was always raised in a smoking environment and just thought it was no real big deal to start. Then I started to drink here and there and smoke pot. Part of me wanted to see what was so enticing to my mom, why she chose that over family. Even after doing it, I couldn't understand.

It seemed to be a waste of time and I certainly didn't like the way I felt the day after. Smoking however became a crutch for me as it helped me with my stress. That was probably an illusion of mine, but nonetheless, a bad habit I picked up along the way.

I hid everything from everyone. Nobody knew my mom was in rehab, nobody even knew what was going on in my home. I wouldn't have many people over my house anyway that's for certain. I didn't want anyone to know. I wasn't the type of person to sit and complain about my life. Complaining wasn't an action to me. I wasn't going to spend my fun time away from the house complaining about the stuff going on inside the house.

I didn't hide my family life intentionally from friends, from school, or anything like that. I just wasn't close enough to anyone to share my life with on that level. There was nobody around to trust with that information. Her family knew about what was going on, but nobody talked about it in front of me. Instead of addressing some of the behaviors that they saw or even sitting Judith down for a talk and saying, "Hey, you are messing up here" "Or maybe you have a problem." Instead they just put a band-aid on it and watched it go on its own way.

A lot of people thought Isaac was the "together" person, but he had his own demons. He was a sexually enticed man on the inside. He would have pornos mailed to him and always have a box of nudey magazines on the bedroom floor along with pictures of naked Harley Davidson magazine pictures hung up on the wall. I even caught him on the phone with a phone sex operator.

One time, my mom told me to go in and wake up my Dad, so I innocently opened the door to wake him up and he had fallen asleep masturbating. I ran back to my mom and just told her that maybe she needs to wake him up instead.

Both of them were sexually perverse and didn't have a care in the world that a child was present. One time we went camping when I was little and they came into the little two-man tent we had and started having sex right beside me while I was supposed to be asleep. I was only in grade school when this happened. Unfortunately, it wouldn't be the only time a sexual act would be performed in front of me while they thought I was sleeping. They had no respect at all for my presence. It always made me feel terribly uncomfortable around them, especially because I couldn't say anything to anyone.

Judith got out of rehab and went full force into the meetings, but her sobriety would only last for about 6 months. The craziness started all over again. She picked up right where she left off. She stayed out for a few more months and then went back into AA again. This time she would stick around for a while and really get in to being sober.

My mom has many negative traits, but she also has some very positive traits as well, and that was that no matter what she put her mind to accomplish she could do it. If she wanted to stay sober, she could stay sober. If she wanted to stay drunk, she stayed drunk. Whatever Judith set her mind to achieve, she achieved.

As a result of being sober, she accumulated a large amount of weight, but that was fine at least she was sober. She could focus on other addictions or obsessions after the first year of sobriety was up. Isaac on the other hand was finally taking care of himself. He lost a tremendous amount of weight and was the skinniest he ever had been. He even shaved off his long biker beard and got different glasses and ditched the old heavily tinted "you can't tell that I'm stoned" glasses that he had.

He actually started talking. He started to talk about his feelings, which was a first. Before he started going to Al-Anon, if I could tell you anything at all about my life with Isaac, I would tell you how quiet it was, how little we talked. I would try so hard to get anything out of the guy and he was emotionless. He would say your common things like, "Hi, I'm home." He would ask me where my mom was, but it was all just regular commentary, nothing like, "Are you okay?"

He started opening up a bit. He started asking me to do stuff with him, like go to the beach, or go for a walk. I just loved this. There were so many times that I would just beg someone to go do something with me and there was always some reason why they couldn't. Before, if it wasn't related to either food or alcohol, then we wouldn't do it. Both Judith and Isaac were very inactive. Their energies were focused elsewhere and that was part of the reason.

When you emotionally spend your time worrying or compensating your emotions with excessive eating, everything snowballs. Your self esteem suffers. Your motivation suffers. I knew all of this had to take a toll on them both and I empathized, perhaps too much sometimes.

I felt bad for Isaac. He always tried to avoid fighting and confrontation, but Judith always antagonized someone about something. Then she would feel bad so she would go out driving around, stop at a store, and buy Isaac a little gift to compensate for her behavior. She would buy him a watch or something small, but that was right after she rang your ass out and made you feel like shit. It was right after she took control of the argument that she started. Sure, all you wanted was a resolution, a calming, but there wasn't one. You can't rationalize with an irrational person.

Isaac and I both lived with the "storm." We walked on eggshells all the time. Once Judith entered into sobriety and Isaac was on his own road to recovery, both were working towards changing some much needed patterns. It was a time to focus and look at their selves in a different light. They had been married for about ten or eleven years at this point, so it was a struggle to get rid of the old familiar, but they were putting effort into the relationship and trying to make their lives together better.

After almost a decade of marriage, Isaac knew Judith was unpredictable and Judith knew Isaac's behavior was predictable. She knew how to manipulate anyone, especially her loved ones. She knew what to do, or what to say to yield the result she wanted. You take away the alcohol from the alcoholic and still wind up with just a sober drunk. Old habits can be hard to break even if alcohol is not present.

During this time, you could watch both of them start to go their separate ways. I don't even know if they both realized that I could see that or not, but I could. Isaac was even busier now than ever because he was taking weekend trips out of town with Al-Anon, which was all women, give or take an additional male here or there. Judith was going on her outings as well. So there were times where I would be myself on the weekend.

I felt left out sometimes to be honest. Here I had this sober family that I longed for all my childhood, and then I still wound up being alone. Isaac tried getting me involved with Alateen, but I just was not into it at all. Al-Anon made more sense to me than what Alateen did. In fact he made me go to 3 meetings to try them out. He said, "Go to 3 meetings and then if you don't like them, you don't have to go again." Well I didn't like the meetings at all. Half the time the people there were talking about doing drugs themselves or their current love lives. That's not to say that somewhere out there, this particular organization isn't suitable for others, because I am sure that it is a great support for many, but for me, I just couldn't get in to it.

I still went to meetings on occasion with Isaac though, and we would also attend AA functions as a family which I enjoyed. I can't say it was so much the event that I enjoyed, but the fact that we would go to a "neutral" playing field and be together.

Meanwhile, on the weekends when they would be gone, I would try to find something to do as well. I did go to parties. Some parents allowed their teenagers to drink at home, so they were allowed to throw drinking parties. The parents would even supply the alcohol. I certainly don't agree with that logic as a parent now, nor did I then, but hence I participated.

I had a boyfriend that I dated very briefly. We went to one of these parties together and he took me out back on the side of the house that night and raped me right there in the yard. I had a beer or two, but I wasn't drunk nor was he. I hurt. I had bruises on my thighs, blood in my panties. I never had sex before. I was in tears when I went back into the house. I found an empty room and just started crying.

A few of my girlfriends came in there and asked why I was crying. I told them why, but nobody really believed me. They thought I was drunk and just crying. I was shaking. I think I walked myself home that night, I can't remember very clearly. I was just too shaken up.

I didn't want to get the police involved. I was afraid they wouldn't believe me anyways. I told a neighbor friend though named Kristen and that was it. I saw Jayson though every day at school. I never spoke to him again. He knew what he did. He knew. It was not shortly after karma caught up with him and he was placed away in prison for several charges dealing with weapons and burglary. I never had to see his face again. He would wind up being in prison even after I had graduated college.

A while after the incident, I confided in my mother and told her what happened. Her response was not what you would expect from a mom. She basically just told me that she too was raped her "first time" by a black man. Perhaps she thought I should feel comforted by this, but I wasn't. Instead I wondered what I even accomplished by sharing this with her.

I never knew if she told Isaac about that incident or not, but he never did say anything to me about it. I swear everyone walked around with brooms sweeping life under the carpet. It was like, "If we don't discuss it, it will go away"

After Judith's first year of sobriety, she started doing leads. A lead is when you stand up in front of a bunch of people at a meeting and you talk about what it was like to be an alcoholic, what it was like getting sober, and what your life is like now. Needless to say, she was very good at this. I was always very proud of her for getting humble and getting up on that podium to speak and share her story with others.

Isaac began doing the same thing in Al-Anon. He would go up and speak to groups as well. This was huge for Isaac. He was so quiet and refrained as a person. So for him to get up their and stand before himself and proclaim his emotions was such a major accomplishment for him. I think it really helped him rebuild himself as a dignified man.

I was very proud of both of them. Their growth however would soon mean a dead end for their marriage...

I had bought my first tarot deck at around age 15. I taught myself how to give readings. It was just something I would do for fun for different friends or family. I would ask Isaac and Judith to let me do their cards for them on two separate occasions. Both readings indicated a separation in a relationship. The cards had nothing to do with the question they had asked in their mind, a question I advised them not to tell me. I performed cold readings on them both so that they could not say that I altered the information I told them based on their question.   I would later discover my readings for them were right.

Chapter 5

Come Undone

Even though Judith was sober, her thinking and actions were still inconsistent. Was this the result of long term alcohol and drug abuse? Perhaps, one never could say. She would do odd things, unthoughtful things, that you just wouldn't expect a mother to do to her child, especially her only child.

After Judith was sober for a couple of years she started going to school and got trained to work with handicapped children. Her motivation and desire was very focused at this time. She used her obsessive compulsive trait to yield a positive result instead of negative. I admired her exercising self discipline.

She achieved her certification and started working at an infant's home for handicapped children.

She would stay at this place of employment for about 11 years. It was a hard job and took a very special type of person to do it. I gave her a lot of credit for using her assertiveness to its utmost potential. Her enthusiasm and motivation were very commendable. She even worked her way up to House Manager of the facility.

The children she worked with were so special. I volunteered to work with her on a camping outing with the kids. Some were confined to wheelchairs and others could walk but were handicapped. My heart just opened up to all of them. It was very eye opening to me. Because no matter what their circumstance or challenge, they got up every day and they lived their life the best they could. They smiled.

That was the best thing my mom ever asked me to participate in and I don't even think she realized the greatness in that. Soon after that experience, I quit smoking. It was a habit I needed to break and I did it. It was hard for me because I was a loner and smoking seemed to be my companion. At least I treated it that way. But I realized this was not a good crutch to have and I put effort into quitting and I succeeded. Judith and Isaac were both proud of me as well. Judith even bought me one of the first stuffed animals that I can honestly remember her buying me in a long time. It was a koala bear puppet.

I loved koala bears ever since I was a baby, they always made me smile. And I was so excited about my gift. There was actually thought and meaning behind it and sincerity. I was very proud of it and it was a very unusual gift from my mother. They even gave me a card with a koala bear on it. I kept that card attached to my dresser mirror for the longest time. It was simple, but it meant a lot to me, that they actually stopped to think about something that I worked hard to accomplish.

Later on that year in October I would attend my younger cousin's birthday party. My mom and I would go to it. My mom was really great with other people's kids, but she was hardly the same with me. I always just watched her in amusement, like is this the same person? So we were at my cousin's little party and Judith had a gift wrapped up for her. I had no idea what she bought her, she never did tell me about it. I watched my cousin open her gift and here it was a Koala Bear puppet just like mine. I was like, "oh wow, where did you find a Koala Bear just like mine?"

Judith would say, "Well that is yours, but you don't use it, so I gave that to her." I said, "That was the one stuffed animal you ever really bought me and I always kept that because it was sentimental to me." My poor Aunt Jeanie, she was the one I so respected out of all, it was her daughter, that would get my koala bear. I certainly couldn't take it back from her.

But it would show me just how low Judith was always willing to go. It would show me how quick she could change her feelings about you and how unpredictable she really was. .

I was now embarking on being 16. I was working very hard in high school. I got involved mentoring grade school children during school hours and then tutoring middle school teenagers after school. I also started going to Upward Bound, a program for college bound students, and I was taking classes in high school for college credit. My grade point average was at its highest at a 4.75.

I also was involved with a local contemporary community theater. I worked there for about 4 years after Isaac took me to see my first play called, "You Can't Take It With You." We never went to a theater together before and I was so excited. I wanted to be a part of it. I didn't have money to go see the shows all the time, but I wanted to somehow. I saw a sign asking for volunteers so I called that week. I started out as an usher passing out programs and worked my way up to performing and primarily running the sound for the shows. I worked there on Friday, Saturday, and Sunday. Rehearsals were during the week so I would do those at night after school. Isaac was great as he would help me get to and from the theater.

I was also involved in different groups and clubs at school. I was even a cheerleader for several years and would cheer at a lot of games. I loved opportunity. I loved the challenge of learning something new and most importantly it limited the time I had to sit alone.

I never minded being alone, in fact I was extremely accustomed to it, but being alone all the time isn't healthy either. So I used my home life, my past, as fuel to rise above the situation and constantly try to become a better person. I was hard on myself, but I needed to be. I didn't realize how important my determination would be later on in my life, but I sensed its value.

Judith began losing her weight and feeling better about herself, but the closeness you would expect Isaac and Judith to have now wasn't present. They were growing apart, but Isaac was trying to hold on, and do everything he could to try and keep the relationship going.

Isaac was now working very closely with a woman named Beth who was his sponsor in Al-Anon. A sponsor is someone you can sit with and tell your most intimate details that you couldn't discuss amongst the group. She was a skinny older lady, about 10 years older than Isaac. She had blonde hair, blue eyes and was a teacher at a local school out in the suburbs. I met her on a couple of occasions and thought she was a very kind woman.

She was very good at motivating Isaac to try new things in his life. He started to dress better and even wear cologne. He was actually showering in the evenings and grooming himself. He had a new outlook on life. Judith I'm sure wasn't used to this at all. Here the man she was used to just worked, ate, and slept, and was very hard to get to do anything outside of the home.

Now, he didn't want to be home. He wanted to work regular hours and go out and about. I certainly couldn't blame him. He deserved to have fun and enjoy his life. I respected any man that tolerated some of the things he had to tolerate. He very easily could have walked away so many times in the relationship, but he never did. He didn't have to support me or her, but he chose to, and I admired him for that.

I had dated a lot of different people up to this point, but nothing serious with any of them, mostly just sexual excursions, nothing very caring. There were a few special people I met along the way that were respectful towards me and for that I was grateful for their companionship at the time.

I kept my distance in relationships. I was always up front about not wanting any thing serious. I had a lot of male friends even more so than female friends that I hung around with. I wasn't an extremely clingy woman at all. I wasn't the most lady-like character either. I was up front and honest. I was the way I wanted people to be with me. I wanted people to be real.

The truth is though people can only be to you what they are to themselves. We go around convincing ourselves of our own lies until we believe them and soon we wind up conveying the lie to everyone else.

My intuitions played a big role in my life especially with people I met. I could feel people on the inside all of the time. I had no idea how to shield everyone's energy yet. I was just a steady listener. It allowed me the opportunity to look inside people and remove their outer covering that they portrayed. It made me more empathetic to some. It made me care for others in a way that I could never anticipate.

Certàin people would cross my path and it would be amazing. The toughest of shells would crack before my eyes. I would speak to these people. Sometime closing my eyes, so I could hear and feel what they had to say. Their words would say one thing, but their souls would say another. And once you speak that truth to their physical being out loud, they have no choice but to listen. You pull the insides out of a person to show them what they have. To show them what they themselves acquired, but cannot see.

Their secrets and their words were safe with me. I could not break that trust. I appreciated the privilege I was being allowed. Intuition is a great honor, not only does it provide us paths to solutions, it provides us with the ability to expand through ourselves and through others.

My friend Anna that I went to kindergarten with, asked me to go her high school dance and I did. I was sick with a headache all night, but I still went. She just broke up with her boyfriend so she needed a date. I met all new people. One in particular was her friend's date, Kevin. We talked about music and different bands. He played the bass and guitar and I told him that I was a singer and that I ran sound for the theater. So we had something in common.

I ended up going home after the dance and couldn't handle staying out to party. I was sick with one of my migraines again, so I couldn't wait to get home. Months later I went to watch some bands play at an all-ages show and here Kevin was behind me. We ended up exchanging phone numbers. He was no longer with the girl he was with at the dance.

So we ended up connecting and talking. He didn't drive. Here he had lost his license I think for drinking. So he would walk from the west-side of town all the way to my house on the east-side, which was about a 3 hour walk, and then he would take a taxi cab home.

I wasn't used to anyone doing something like that for me. It goes to show you where my own self-esteem was wounded from growing up with alcoholism. My self worth was just bare. Someone could literally do the smallest of things and I would be entirely grateful.

We dated on and off. There were times in the very beginning that he would stand me up. I should have known then to vacate the relationship, but I always went back. I had such a distorted reality of what love was. Love to me took work, love to me was painful. Love to me meant compromising myself. I had a sick pattern that I myself was raised to believe was right. Thinking back now, I still hadn't acknowledged how sick and unhealthy my family life was, and as a result, I was securing a relationship that would only repeat the past, but in a different context.

Kevin was older than me. I had always dated older men, very rarely someone my own age. I related to them more. I was about 15 when we met and he was 21. He drank and I would drink with him. But I wouldn't drink to get drunk, that was the difference, and he would. He was a very different drunk than I was used to.

I was used to Judith, the obnoxious, loud drunk. She stumbled. She fell. She slurred her words. She pissed herself. Kevin was the complete opposite. If he drank all day and I was unaware of him doing so, I could hardly tell at all that he was drunk, besides for some erratic things that he might say to me. He didn't slur his words. He didn't stagger. His eyes weren't glazed over. He was still kept together, but if you were close to him as a person, you would be able to tell, as he would belittle you in front of anyone.

When we first started dating, we would only see each other over the weekends. I had a very busy schedule and he worked at a local plating company so he was working all week. We would talk though almost every day in between my different activities. So I never saw the pattern full blown. One of the times we went out to a band practice place. They were old office turned into rehearsal halls for different music groups to practice. So we hung out there. I had no idea he had been drinking all day before we even got there at night.

We were alone and he just freaked out and threw me into the door. When Kevin was 16, he was into cocaine and had a problem with it. He had an alcoholic mother as well that reminded you of the actress that played in "Mommie Dearest." She was a sweet woman, but a time bomb waiting to explode.

After Kevin lashed out on me, he broke down in tears and started to tell me how his mom would hit him all the time when he was little. I felt bad for him. I wanted to make things better for him. I felt bad for the life he had and the choices he made. What I failed to realize was that these choices were made by him, not by me. We can't prevent someone from a falling grace. We can't fix the broken. Perhaps we can be temporary band-aids for the grief, but we are not the solution.

The longer we dated, the more entangled I felt. My family actually liked the guy which was a rarity. He had a job which was of high importance to them. This was as far as I had ever gone in a relationship so I felt I had some sort of stock reserved. Plus, he was the only one I felt I could trust. Perhaps at the time, this was very true.

Nobody knew all about me. I wouldn't tell someone something unless they asked. I had this distance I would keep with people. If I didn't get close to them, I wouldn't get hurt. It was a defense mechanism that I picked up to cope with my family life. For me it was a survival method.

So Kevin broke the barrier. I gave myself unto him fully and for the most part he gave himself to me, so I thought. We had a common pain and we shared that bond together. That Christmas he proposed to me. I never had anyone propose to me. I never had anyone actually want to commit to me in this way. This was all very strange and foreign. So I had said yes.

Knowing what I know now, I can look back and see all the warning signs were there for me not to continue the relationship. However, I still had a lot of personal growth and reality that I needed to address in my life before I would realize this.

He was truly placed in my life to get me sick enough to get better. I had a lot of un-doings that I needed to manifest from the way I was raised, but I did not realize at what magnitude until later on.

I ended up calling the engagement off. My instincts were there about the relationship, but I still felt terrible about breaking it off with him. He was controlling even then which was very overbearing for me. I felt overwhelmed.

Meanwhile, my family life was becoming more unstable. Judith was acting very weird. She kept lying and saying her back was bothering her, and she needed to sleep on a cot in the living room. So we borrowed a cot from my grandparents and put it in the living room for Judith. She was no longer sleeping in the same bed with Isaac. If she was home, she made sure that she was occupied on the phone with someone to avoid any confrontation with me or with Isaac.

She used meetings as a scapegoat to get out of the house. She wasn't talking to me at all. On New Years Eve of 1992, we wanted her to go to First Night Erie with us. She refused to spend New Years Eve with us. Isaac and Judith both argued. It was very sad. So Isaac and I went to the First Night Erie by ourselves. I think later on he met up with Beth and I went over to a friend's house.

I certainly wasn't in to drinking away sadness, it never worked for me. In fact, I didn't feel like drinking at all that night. I just had this pit in my stomach. This was a different kind of feeling too. My mother was going to do something, but I wasn't sure what.

Not long after that New Years Eve, I came home from school and caught her. Our walls were bare. A lot of our belongings were just gone. Only thing left was the dust in the corners. And there she was, caught red handed. I scared the shit out of her. She turned around and I said, "What are you doing?"

"I'm leaving," she said. She didn't offer to take me with her. She didn't offer much of an explanation. It all happened so quickly, within 5 minutes of me being home she was gone. I was thrown off guard. I just started crying as I stared at all the empty space. She even took some of my stuff with her so she could pawn it for money at the local pawn shop. She took my television and my keyboard that they bought me for Christmas. There were other odd things she took too, but I was so shocked I can't even recall everything. None of that stuff mattered anyways.

Not even 10 minutes had passed and the phone rang. I answered it not knowing who was on the other end. I said, "Hello," the male voice said, "Is Isaac there?" I said, "No, I'm sorry he is still at work, can I tell him who is calling?" "Just tell him Patrick called." He even said his last name and my stomach sank to the floor, it was my biological father. I never in my life spoke to him until that very moment. And I think he knew who I was. I think he felt who I was.

I didn't know what to think. I looked out the door, "Was someone watching me?" How could this timing be any more perfect? I called my Aunt Peggy and told her he called, she must have called Isaac right away, because he came home within 10 minutes, and Patrick called back right after he walked in the door.

They talked briefly. I was so curious I could have crawled out of my skin. My curiosity was quickly discouraged by anyone around me. I think they killed my curiosity with fear. They tried to anyways, but I could never help to wonder.

No matter how crazy and mental they told me my father was, I some how felt he was more intuitive than anything. Did his intuition scare him or others? Did he drink to numb what he felt or known? I don't know. Whatever it was, nobody wanted him near me or me near him. They allowed so many other things to go on in my life, but when it came down to Patrick, all of a sudden people got protective or cautious. It was rather amusing.

So why did Patrick call only minutes after Judith left Isaac and I and moved out? I don't know, but maybe he felt my energy from afar, my sadness as I watched a woman walk out of the house I grew up in, and never look back.

After Isaac got off the phone, he had a chance to take a good look around and see what just took place. "She's gone," I said. Isaac asked, "Did she explain anything to you or give you an idea where she is going to be at?" "No." I said. "Did she even give you her phone number?" "No, nothing," I said.

I think it would be 6-9 months before I ever saw her again. She called to speak to Isaac about finances, but never spoke to me. Isaac would plead with her to talk to me, but she wouldn't, finally one time she did, but I still didn't see her for some time afterwards.

Here I was being left with some poor guy that didn't even conceive me. He knew I had no place to go. Isaac and Beth were always together soon after all this went down. Ironically, Beth left her husband that was in AA after a very long marriage. I can't recall if it was before or after Judith left, I'm not sure.

Judith always told me years later that there were rumors going around about Isaac and Beth having a relationship with one another. Granted though, Judith was always jealous of the bond that they had. Isaac wouldn't talk to Judith about intimate emotions. I don't even know if he did, if Judith would have even listened.

Judith also at one point told Isaac that she never really loved him, that she just knew he was someone stable to have around to help her support herself and her child. She told him that she always really viewed their relationship as a friendship.

Maybe Isaac did cheat on Judith with Beth, there is a possibility, but I certainly couldn't blame him. Having to tolerate emotional and even physical abuse from Judith for 13 years, I could understand why. I wanted more than anything for him to be happy and enjoy his life.

Years later, I would find sheets of paper tucked away in an old desk we had that Isaac wrote on, that would indicate there was a relationship with Beth prior to his divorce, but again, I could never blame him.

Beth was the polar opposite of Judith. She was active, loving, and would always be willing to help Isaac make improvements with himself or his surroundings. She was very caring. She would bake things for Isaac and he just loved it. They would exercise together, go see shows together. They were certainly two people journeying together after having both dealt with alcoholic partners most of their life. They were now able to just enjoy this new freedom.

Meanwhile, I was left alone a lot. With this new found relationship Isaac got involved with, there was little time for me. We would still go grocery shopping together every week and he would take me to get a bite to eat here and there. At this time, we still lived together and Beth lived in an apartment so he was good about prioritizing and telling her, "No, I'm going to go take my daughter here." He always made a point to try and include me or fit me in wherever he could.

I cared very deeply for Isaac and respected him for taking me into his home and allowing me to live with him. He may have not always been emotionally there for me up to this point, but our relationship as a father and daughter was present.

Also, during this time my Aunt Jeanie who was working very hard at the local hospital to support their then, two kids, encouraged Joel, her husband who did not work, to get me out of the house. So he started asking me to go have coffee. I think he was in his 30's at the time. I trusted Jeanie, so I automatically trusted Joel.

He was educated, a very loving father, and loyal husband. I had no reason to ever think otherwise. So during the day, he would offer to take me to different cafes and we would have coffee and dessert. Jeanie wanted someone to be with me during this time as Judith was gone already and Isaac wasn't around much.

We would sit and talk. He would talk to me about Judith and how messed up she always was and how her leaving was a surprise. I felt okay talking to him, he seemed like he cared about my situation, but then he started getting very weird rather quickly.

He began showing up at my house unannounced. He was smart. He knew when nobody was home. It was a cold day the one time he came over. This time that we went out would be the last time I would ever go out with him. He thought we would drive out to the peninsula and look at the lake. This was a much longer drive than what we would normally take. He would start asking me sexual questions. He would tell me about dreams that he had of me performing sexual acts on him. He would start telling me about different sexual things about him and my Aunt, and other women he was with in college before they were married.

He started asking me if I was in this porno he watched and if I had any tattoos on me. He swore I looked like this one porno star in the movie he rented at the adult book store in Erie. I was like, "No, and I don't have any tattoos at all." He started asking to see my bra and I said, "No, you are married to my aunt, what are you talking about?" He kept begging me, "Come on, just let me see the strap. That's it." I said, "No."

About this time I was getting a little nervous. My heart began pounding in my chest. He was driving us into the back of the Coast Guard Center which was desolate and no traffic at all was present. He was getting frustrated with me because I wasn't complying with him. So he pulled over by a restroom. He came back about five minutes later, with liquid all down his pants right by his crotch. He got in the truck and I said, "I think you should take me home now." It would be a long time before I made it home.

Now, he started telling me, "If you ever tell Jeanie about this, she will never believe you, because I will tell her it was all your fault, and she will believe me." He wasn't going to take me home until I promised that I wouldn't tell her. I was nervous and in shock about the whole situation. He started driving around on all these side streets out in the middle of the country. I had no idea where I was at all. I had thought about jumping out of the moving truck, but then was afraid because I was surrounded by just corn fields.

If I was to jump out, he would likely catch me, and there was nobody out there to hear me at all. He told me about a gun he kept under the backseat. I don't know why he told me this either, I just tried to keep my head on no matter what he did or said. I just kept pacifying him, reassuring that I wouldn't say anything.

Finally, once he was convinced, he took me home. I was so shaken up when I got home, I felt terrible.

If there was one person I respected the most it was Jeanie. She was a hard worker, a loyal and caring woman. She was also pregnant at the time. If I told her this, it would either ruin her family, or destroy my relationship with her. I ended up confiding in her sister Peggy.

Peggy and Jeanie were the closest people I had. Peggy and her husband Arnold always invited me over to their house. Her husband Arnold actually tricked me to sing on his music tracks, and then I slowly got comfortable singing in front of him, so we would make several songs together. I loved it.

I told Peggy about what Joel did and she told Arnold. He was infuriated. Peggy basically told me to just stay away from him. I was hushed again. I would have to attend family gatherings, interact with my Aunt Jeanie, and her children, and act like nothing ever happened.

I even confided in Kevin about this and he would turn the tables on me, and tell me that I probably instigated Joel and made him act that way. I got so fed up with nobody believing the truth.

My relationship with Kevin was still on and off. I wasn't good at commitments. It was difficult for me to let myself get close to anyone, especially, actually being with the same person. I had bypassed relationships by keeping them short. I could still have the pleasure of getting slightly close to someone, but would always end the relationship before it evolved to a different level. It was a defense mechanism I had.

Months after my incident with Joel, I decided to go to a Super Bowl Party held at a friend's house blocks away from my home. It was just a bunch of us hanging out watching the game. I wore an old beat up sweatshirt and a pair of sweat shorts, nothing real fancy at all that day. I was just kind of emotionally exhausted from the past few months that I just felt like bumming around and relaxing.

When the game was over, I was going to walk myself home, but it was dark out. My friend Roy advised that I should let his older brother give me a ride home instead of walking by myself this late at night. So after much convincing, I took him up on the offer.

Roy's brother, Butch, was in his mid 20's. He had dark hair and was tall with a medium build. We got in the car and he told me he just had to stop and get something at his house which was only blocks away. So I said that was fine, I knew where Roy lived so I was familiar with the route. We got there and went to the door that led to the basement. Once I was inside that was it, a different person stood before me.

I was thrown down on the bed and my shorts were slid open. He was full force on top of me holding my hands down. I kept trying to get up. Then he started clenching my neck while raping me. I was blurring out, my body was there, but my spirit was elsewhere. I remember only bits and pieces. I remember him yelling at me, "You like that, Don't you!" His sexual rage was unpredictable. I just trembled. His lips were slobbering all over my face and suffocating me at the same time. The more I fought him, the more turned on he became.

He wanted to beat the shit out of me. You could tell. His rage was so real. The fire in his eyes was just there. I just tried to keep my composure. I yelled and then he slapped me across my face and covered my mouth.

When he was done, it was over. I don't remember how I got home. It wasn't that I was intoxicated or anything like that, it was my own body trying to recover. I just remember coming home to an empty house that night and being scared. The first thing I did was shower. I wanted to wash this stench of a man off of me.

That night and that morning, I was sicker than a dog. Any time I got so emotionally upset, my body would just shut down. I was sick to my stomach all day. I even slept on the couch downstairs instead of my room. Then the phone rang. I just let the answering machine get it, and it was Butch. Somehow he got my phone number. He said, "I just wanted to let you know I had a really good time last night, we'll have to do that again," and hung up.

Did I ever go to the cops? No, not at all. The thought crossed my mind, but at the same time, I just felt like nobody was going to believe me. I knew the way the system was there and it wasn't going to be worth the battle. I walked away with my life and was grateful for that.

I did confide in my friends that were there at the Super Bowl party. My friend Danny that I was close with told me that Butch even came back to the house that night and told everybody that I gave him a blow job and that was all we did. I was enraged that this man had the audacity to go tell my friends this. I told Danny what happened and he was just shocked, but again, nobody would really say anything about it.

Months later, Danny would come back to me and tell me that Butch was sent to the Florida penitentiary. He was considered so violent and dangerous that they didn't want him even residing in the same state where he was being charged. He almost killed his own girlfriend of several years. She was pregnant with his baby. He beat the shit out of her so bad that the baby drowned in its own blood.

Somewhere in between, I met Nolan. He lived a few blocks away from me and was the same age as me. He was a guitarist. He had what I called a "stable" family, two brothers, nice big house, and two parents. He was very goal and friend oriented. He had a group of friends he would hang out with for many years. The opposite of me, I was nomadic. I didn't have one set of people I hung out with. I would just come and go in and out of many different groups, no real set of friends.

Him and I would go out to playgrounds together at night and sit there and talk. I always had so much respect for him. He was "untouched," never had sex yet, and I thought that was beautiful. I guess that was what was so great about our relationship was that it was not based on sex, like all of my other relationships. I respected him so much that it was difficult for me to be intimate with him. He was nice to me and he actually had cared for me in a different way than what I had been shown.

I had broken it off with Kevin again at one point and this was going to be it for me. It was not long after, that I got an urgent message on our answering machine from his sister-in-law. He was in the hospital in critical condition. He was having issues with his heart and had to have an emergency surgery right away. It was very serious.

I made arrangements to go see him at the hospital. I felt so bad, because I broke up with him days or a week prior. Everyone was saying, I literally "broke" his heart. I sat with him and I held his hand. The Priest came into the hospital room to read him his last rights. My emotions were tremendous at this moment. I told him that we were going to get through this.

This just got me on a whole different level with him. I felt terrible about the entire situation. I felt guilty too. Even though this wasn't my fault for him being in the hospital, I felt it was in the back of my mind. His family knew how much I meant to Kevin and when I got out of the relationship, they had a lot to say to me about it. Had I known what I do now, I would have placed everything into perspective a lot sooner, but I had so much to learn still. So after Kevin's surgery, we were soon back together.

I wanted to be good at a relationship. I was so come and go with everyone, never getting close to them, that I was trying to change, and really put some effort into this relationship. I guess in a sense I was afraid nobody would ever love me like Kevin. I had such a distorted sense of self worth that I actually honestly thought that. I thought "this" was it.

In hindsight, this relationship didn't even fit into my personal goals. I wanted to get out of Erie ever since I was little, but Kevin had roots in Erie and wasn't going to move away from them. He relied too heavily on the network of friends and family. Nolan was the same way, he was embedded in Erie and never wanted to move away either.

For as long as Isaac could remember I wanted out of Erie. I just had to do the footwork to better myself to get out. That would be slightly put on hold when I got fully involved with Kevin. Everything was okay when I lived with Isaac. I had that boundary between Kevin and I that placed me in the driver's seat. I wasn't in Kevin's realm just yet.

At this time, I went to a career counselor before I was getting ready to graduate high school, I would find out about another hurdle I needed to get over in order to go to college. I worked very hard in school, earned college credits, and always was striving to go to college. I thought that my academic excellences and honor enrollment would assist in some sort of scholarship for college, but I was in for a big surprise.

I wanted to go to Pittsburgh University outside of Erie. I was accepted and everything, but could not get the financing to go. The guidance counselor at my high school advised me that I would have to take a year off because I was still on my parents taxes so my financial information was going by their income, not mine. And the honest truth was nobody was going to pay for my education.

Isaac told me he would help me financially if I went to a state college, the same college Beth went too. I didn't want to go there though, as it was known as being a big party school. Plus the major issue was it was not going to accept the over 40 college credits I had acquired in high school. So Isaac was upset with me for not wanting to attend Beth's old college.

There was a college downtown in Erie that would accept my credits. It was a private college so the cost was a lot higher in range. How was I to achieve this? I didn't know. I said to my counselor, "There has got to be something I can do to get myself declared independent." And there was. I would need to go in front of the school board and show them that I should be emancipated from my parents. In order to do this though, I needed to live on my own and work.

I went out and got a retail job, which I couldn't stand but it was a quick employment and under a mile away from Isaac's house. I worked there and saved my money and then started looking for an apartment. By this time, I was in contact with Judith who knew an apartment manager in AA that had vacancies. There was a little apartment on 130 Hill Road for $150 a month including utilities. I wanted this. It was so small, but I wanted it. Mind you I was still going to high school and working right after school. It would be a schedule I would keep for several months which was very exhausting.

So I told Kevin I was going to move out and he told me he wanted to move out of his parent's house as well, so we wound up moving in together. This was how I would be able to emancipate myself and be declared independent and it worked. I was granted emancipation at age 17. Now I would be able to work for a year, file my own taxes, and apply for college the following fall.

Chapter 6

130 Hill Road

Kevin and I were living at our new little place together. It was exciting and I was nervous as well. Isaac would invite us over for dinner on occasion and would take us to the grocery store. One time I cashed my check at work, hopped in the car, gave the cash to Kevin, and we drove across the parking lot to the grocery store and he swore he lost the money. I would realize later on, that this was never true. My whole check was taken right before my eyes. We looked everywhere for it and it was never found. These little instances would build up over time and make more sense, the more involved we became.

Shortly after I graduated high school I got a better job at a new place that was just opening up. It was a grocery store, but it paid a lot more than what I was making in retail. I applied for the bakery. I wanted to be a cake decorator in the worst way. They told me I had to start out as a clerk first and then they would see. I bugged the manager constantly about showing me how to decorate, even asked to take some tools home to practice, and they let me. I ended up being one of the top decorators there. I loved my job because I got to do art. I would wind up keeping that job for the longest out of all jobs.

Living with Kevin changed the dynamics of our relationship in a lot of ways. I didn't have that boundary there anymore that I had when I lived with Isaac. I got to see what he was really like on all angles and got to see my own angles as well. I wasn't perfect. I would never claim perfection even now. I was learning how to live with someone. Even though I lived with Isaac, we were not up in each other's faces all the time. Kevin and I weren't around each other constantly either. He was a musician so he had band practices, plus he would work 3rd shift and I would work 2nd shift.

The times we were together, arguments would always arise. He would even have outbursts at a store out in public. One time he started yelling at me right in front of the cashier about some bread I bought and how I should know better. He went on so much that I had to leave the store. And if he knew he was starting to push your buttons, he would keep doing it even more. He grabbed the groceries and chased me out of the store still yelling at me. What was even more embarrassing was that this was where I worked.

The emotional abuse was very fast progressing. I started getting sick a lot. On the weekends he would want to party and I just wasn't into it, but would try to be. If anyone tried to call me, especially if it was a male, he would freak out. He would even start saying rude comments while I was on the phone with them. He was very manipulative. Eventually everyone stopped calling me. They were probably afraid to get me into trouble.

If I went to go get coffee with a co-worker, I would have to tell him who was there, if there were any guys there, if I talked to any of them, if I did, what did I say? I would be interrogated for sometimes hours. I would end up in tears and wind up getting myself sick the next day or so with a migraine. Everything started out subtle, but gradually got to be more enduring as the days progressed.

My life was totally out of character. I was always independent, assertive, and goal oriented. He would talk down to me so much that I finally started to believe him. I became scared to do anything. Plus he was a closet drinker. He would drink here and there around me, but he really drank on his own time. I would find empty beer bottles shoved away in the trash can. Again a lot different from Judith who was blatantly open about drinking and didn't give a crap who she drank in front of or where, so as long as she was drinking.

Every time he would drink, an argument was sure to follow, but then once we would arrive at our destination or get around others, it was like someone flipped a switch on him, and then he would be nice as could be. That was why nobody knew what was going on.

I kept a journal, but again had to censor my thoughts and feelings because he would read everything I wrote. If I asked him not to, he would take immediate offense and insist I wrote something bad about him. Everything I did was monitored carefully.

Even phone conversations with family members were monitored. He always had to be present to hear exactly what I was saying to make sure I didn't say anything out of context to indicate how crazy our lives together truly were. Even if I said everything was all good to someone, he would instigate that. I couldn't win.

Little did I realize how I was repeating the pattern played out all my life. I was reenacting my past without even knowing. I would play the same role I always did, just a different character.

My migraines and sickness worsened terribly. Every week I was sick. My nerves were just shot. I had no space at all and couldn't go anywhere by myself except for work. I was constantly blamed for cheating and being unfaithful even though my life consisted of working and waiting at home alone for him.

I had to go to the doctor on several occasions to help with the migraines. Now I know that my body was physically alerting me to get out of the situation I was in, but at the time I listened to those around me insisting it was medical. They gave me blood pressure medicine and some pills to take at the sign of a migraine which helped, but didn't stop the insanity at home. The blood pressure medicine was terrible. I started getting anxiety attacks.

I would never wish anxiety attacks on anyone, they are not fun. You feel nervous to do anything in life, even simple chores. Arguments between Kevin and I would worsen. I had no way of regrouping myself. If I went into the bathroom to get a moment to myself in a heated argument, he would throw open the door and keep yelling at me.

So what was there that was good? The only time we were able to get along was during our sexual endeavors. It was the only time we didn't argue.

It was very sick and twisted and mimicked Isaac and Judith's bond, their sexual sickness with one another. It was the only thing they could do and not argue about. I remember countless of times them having sex right in front of me, so drunk they were oblivious to the fact that I was awake.

I remember Judith in our hotel room at Disneyland on our first "real" family vacation, she started giving Isaac a blow job right in the bed beside me. I remember the constant moans I heard of them in the bedroom downstairs at our house. It was sick and I had no idea just to what level of sickness it was.

I would find pictures that they would take of themselves performing various sexual things. I would find my mom's dildo in her drawer and a stash of porns in the top closet.

Here I was in a relationship that revolved around the same thing. Sure it wasn't as extreme as Isaac and Judith, but the same laws were applying. I wasn't having sex in front of other people. I wasn't sitting there watching pornography or playing with sex toys either, but what I was doing was basing my closeness with another person not on what we had in common, but the sexual relationship we had. I thought I was making love to someone that loved me. I trusted Kevin. In my own sickness, when he told me he loved me, I believed him. My perceptions were very far off.

Where was Judith during all of this? She ended up meeting another man named Brock who was from Waterford. He was a very tall skinny man who was also a recovering alcoholic. He was slow in his speech, had long brown hair, and wore glasses. She ended up moving in with him and living out in Waterford in a trailer.

I was still fighting to have a loving relationship with her, but between work and her new boyfriend, it was hard to fit me in. I have to laugh because even as jacked up as Kevin was, even he would get disappointed over Judith's relationship with me. There were countless times I would call her to make arrangements for us to go do something and she would cancel at the last minute or never show, and mind you she was in sobriety at the time.

I would just be so disappointed and Kevin knew that. His family had an alcoholic mother, but they always stuck by one another. They were intricate and detailed and supported each other, even with the mother's shortcoming.

As time went on, I bought our first car. Kevin's Dad would co-sign the loan for me. My own parents had refused my request for help when I asked them to co-sign, so Ron, Kevin's Dad trusted me enough to help.

Kevin brought a white Monte Carlo into our relationship when we first moved in together and the thing was a piece of shit. The brake fluid always leaked out of it, so we were constantly losing our brakes when we were out on the road. The car had no heat or defrost, so in the middle of winter he drove me to work with the windows down just so he could see the road.

We got the new car in May of 1994. Kevin's birthday was May 8th. The night before his birthday, he was going to go out with his friend from work. I made plans to go over to Judith and Brock's house to do laundry and have dinner. When I came home, Kevin wasn't even there, the car wasn't there either.

I had a birthday party and dinner planned for him at Isaac's house and he didn't call or show up at all. I was devastated. Judith and I went to my grandma's house and I just cried, this was a major turning point for me. He was out driving the new car drunk and stayed over someone's house.

I ended up grabbing some of my belongings and staying with Isaac again. I left the car with Kevin. I didn't have a driver's license yet, and he used the car to get to work, so I left it with him. I started going to Al-Anon with Isaac. I started to realize the patterns that were resurfacing in my own life that stemmed from my life with Judith. Al-Anon would be a stepping stone for me to break out of the cycle. It also introduced me to a beautiful older woman named Suzanne.

I always loved her energy. She was a calm woman and spoke with great clarity. She would become my confidant for many years. She would listen to me and not judge a word that I said. She was neutral. She wasn't related to me nor did she have any motive to betray me. She was just Suzanne.

For the first time in my life, I had someone to validate my thoughts and feelings. Our conversations allowed me to uncover a lot of hidden grief. Having someone from the outside look in, gave me insight to a whole different perspective of my life. It was like, "What, you mean this isn't normal?" My instincts and intuitions were there, but I didn't have anyone to reinforce them, or anyone to say, "You know what, you are right." I was surrounded by people that were constantly telling me I was wrong.

Even Isaac and Beth were very supportive during this time. I remember Isaac telling me he had no idea that all of this was going on. He said, "I just always noticed if we had dinner and were you talked about something you knew, Kevin would argue with you that you were wrong." And that was how it was, always arguing, always something wrong. I don't know if he had a fear of me being smarter than him or if he just never wanted to look stupid. Whatever the issue was, it became a deep insecurity of his that he constantly sought to defend.

I'll never forget one time I bought two 50 cent washcloths for our apartment and he had a fit that I would even buy those. I bought myself a pair of shoes for 5 dollars and he had a fit over that as well, but he would be able to buy himself whatever he wanted. If he needed or wanted to spend $200 on speakers, he would do it in a heartbeat.

I worked too, but there was a double standard. I paid all our bills and was the one to manage our bank account we had together. I even had money saved up in the bank. After I moved in with Isaac, I gave Kevin the checks to pay the bills, and he never did. Instead he pulled all the money out of our account. I went to go close the bank account one day and all the cash was gone, nothing left at all.

Kevin tried to convince me that he spent the money on a walkman for me, but I wasn't going for it. I was starting to catch on… finally. I remember one time I was paying our phone bill and saw a high charge for a call made on our phone. Here it was some phone sex thing he called while I wasn't home. He swore he didn't do it, but everything was starting to add up.

My intuitions were peeking through. One night I woke up startled at 3 in the morning at Isaac's house. I could see Kevin being chased by the cops and getting pulled over, then being taken away. I didn't hear from Kevin for a few days after I had that vision. Then when I did see him, I told him about my vision and asked him if there was anything he needed to tell me.

Here he was playing a show in Cleveland, OH and went to drive home after he had been drinking and got pulled over by the cops. He had to spend a night in jail and got a fine on top of that for DUI. He wasn't going to tell me, but once I told him my vision, he sat there with a guilty look on his face and then confessed.

I never once hated Kevin. No matter what he did, I never hated him. For some reason, I felt just bad for him, but I should have applied that to myself. He was the only person I had a history with for so many years that I kept trying to make things "work" for us, but they never did. We even tried marriage counseling, but the end result was we were two entirely different people.

He would mess up and then try really hard to make things right, but it just didn't work. We paid for a vacation together with his brother and sister-in-law down in Duck, North Carolina. We rented a house there with them. I had the option of going to Cleveland to go to a concert with some friends or to go to Duck. After much convincing from Kevin, I went to Duck.

The distance between us was there though. I could feel that. I was starting to become aware. When I was with him, I would be sick. When I was by myself, my health reflected it, and I wasn't sick. There was no denying that my body was physically signaling me.

When we went to drive home, I drove, but only had a driver's permit. It was very early about 3AM or so when we left. I wound up getting into an accident in Virginia. I totaled the car. I just lost control of the wheel and started fish tailing down the road.

I felt horrible about the accident, but Kevin ended up getting a new car, and our insurance paid off the old loan, which had my name attached to it, so everything worked out for the best. So that was interesting how life worked. Meanwhile, back in Erie, the friends that I was supposed to go to the concert with, got hit by a semi truck, killed the two people in the back instantly. That would have been me, if I would have chosen to go.

After our trip, we both started venturing off seeing other people. I was slowly getting the courage to explore what was out there and not confining myself anymore to one place or one person. During my relationship with Kevin I was so delusional with what "love" truly was and the nature of which it comes.

Why did I keep going back? The same reason I kept loving and supporting my mom no matter what she did to me or around me. I believed in unconditional love even if it affected my own physical or emotional self. What was unfortunate though is that just like my mother, Kevin would also take advantage of my sincerity to him.

What is even sicker is that while I would be getting the courage to venture away from Kevin, Judith began meddling in the situation. One time I went out to her trailer to spend time with her and Brock. She invited Kevin over and never told me until it was too late and I was already there, with no way home.

She always told me, "Why can't you love Kevin?" I said, "Cause he is an alcoholic." She would say, "I'm an alcoholic and you love me?" She was right that I did love her regardless, but that was because she was my mom. I had respect for her, even if she didn't have respect for me.

I started getting involved in outside activities to try and re-focus myself again and gain back the control I surrendered to someone else. I was invited to do a radio show with a girl I met. She worked at the college radio station in downtown Erie. This would inspire me to major in Communication Arts at the same university.

I would apply to college to attend that Fall. I was still told there was no way to get funding to attend and this time I was being told directly by the Admissions Board.

Three days before classes were to begin, I woke up abruptly at 5am. I had a vision and I was told to go through the garbage can. So I ran downstairs immediately. Isaac said, "What in the world are you doing? I told him, "I'm going to college." He said, "You can't go, they already told you no." I dug through the trash frantically and said, "They made a mistake."

I found my Financial Forms in the trash and my vision was right, I checked where I was shown in my vision and the income was wrong! They made a mistake on the calculations! That's why I wasn't able to go. Isaac still thought I was out of my mind.

I went down and showed that same Financial Officer that told me there was no way possible for me to attend classes and showed him the miscalculation. He called several other people while I was present and they confirmed the mistake. I met with the chairperson of the Communication Arts Department and started class only days later. I was ecstatic!

The more I achieved the angrier that made Kevin. I could always do a lot of different things and enjoyed that part of my life very much, but he did not like to be overshadowed. It made him look bad. He didn't like to feel stupid, so by exhibiting control over someone else, it made him feel in control of himself.

Perfect example was me working for the radio station there. I always offered to help the bands out that he was in because we would play local bands on the air, but he never once would get humble and let me do it. He would let someone else play their music, but never me.

I also became the Promotions Director of the station as well as being a personality. I started out doing news copy and I was terrible at that! The poor guy Timmy that trained me was so nervous around girls that while I was reading on LIVE air about a tragic plane accident, he dropped his papers, and got hung up in my headphone wire, and pulled his own headset off in the process. I started laughing uncontrollably, while I was reading something so serious.

So eventually I met my radio partner Shanna. We would fall into this radio show together by accident. She started out doing news too and was also a

Communication Arts Major. The guy that trained us to actually run the board showed us a few things and then left. Here we were, alone on air, together. It was hilarious.

We would be known as the "Redhead Leading The Blonde" which eventually changed to the "Blonde Leading The Blonde," after I cut off my hair to my shoulders and went blonde. I loved doing radio, it was a real way for me to deal with the stress I had in my life. Again, nobody really knew everything that was going on. All they knew is that when I had to do a job, I did it with a smile on my face, and I did it to the best of my ability.

I would have a dream of a psychic woman that I would visit. She was a larger woman with short hair. She had some information for me and for the path that was ahead. The next day when I awoke, I found out a psychic fair was coming to Erie. My friend that I told about my dream would go with me to get a reading.

We walked in to the conference area and way in the back, I saw her. I saw the woman in my dream. I walked straight towards her without any hesitation. I sat down in the chair across from her and said nothing.

I never visited a psychic before. It was only my dream that prompted me to do so. I was skeptical. The first thing she said to me though right after I sat down, "You are very psychic yourself." Nobody had ever acknowledged me in that way before. I don't even believe I acknowledged myself in that light.

She was warning me of a tragedy ahead, an unavoidable tragedy. It was one that needed to occur to finally denote an end to a particular phase in my life. I asked her about my relationship and she said the most valuable answer to me, "If you have to ask the question, you already know the answer." And I did, I knew my answer.

After I just started college, it would be months later that I found out I was pregnant. I had no idea what to do. I had just started college, something I had worked so very hard to achieve. I was very stunned. Kevin and I were still on again and I told him that I was pregnant. After I did that, everything changed. All of a sudden he didn't want much of anything to do with me. I would try to get him to go to doctor's appointments with me and he would say he had to work late. Then I would call him from the doctor's office, and his co-worker would tell me he actually left early.

He would wind up getting involved with a stripper named "Sunshine." I remember his sister-in-law telling me that he brought Sunshine over to the family and she told Kevin, "Stick with me and you'll see a rainbow." While we were trying to work things out, I pulled down the visor in the car and her stripper picture flew down onto my lap. That would be the woman he would be with while I was at the doctor's office.

Then I had told Isaac about my pregnancy and he was very quiet about it. He was not comfortable with this at all. Eventually he told me that if I was to keep this baby that I couldn't live with him because he couldn't help support the two of us. I would obviously never expect him to financially support me and a child, but the living arrangement was a shock. I had nobody I could stay with.

Judith who got her tubes tied after she birthed me could never bare a child to any man going forward, so she saw this as an opportunity. She told me, "You could give the baby over to Brock and I, and we could raise the child as our own, and you would always know where it was at." This made my blood curdle. There was no way in hell that I would as so much allow that woman to even attempt raising another child. Absolutely not! She offered to take my baby before she offered me a roof over my head, that disgusted me.

I was extremely stressed and very alone. Not to mention that once people started finding out about it at college, none of my new so-called "friends" would have anything to do with me. I wasn't eating right. I had a college school load on me and was still working at the bakery to pay for my school books. I started having sharp pains in my abdomen and started bleeding. I would be taken to the emergency room on several occasions due to this. I was even put on "bed rest," but I couldn't be off from school.

I was terribly sick so I couldn't even keep food down at all and the bleeding would continue. I remember I walked up to our old apartment where Kevin still lived and climbed through the window. It was the only time in my life I had suicidal thoughts. I looked at our old place, I looked at our pictures. I looked at my new mother pamphlets. I just cried.

Something told me to look under the bed. And there were pictures of an old trip that Kevin took to a best friend of his down in Texas. I totally trusted him on this trip that he took for a week and never questioned him about it. I would see these pictures of him with another woman at some club they were at. He hid them all this time.

I would hear a message on his voicemail from his new girlfriend. I took my rings off that he gave me and left them there. My thoughts were so deranged.

Everything was surfacing. It wasn't just about Kevin, it wasn't just about me, or just about being pregnant. It was about my life up to this point. It was about me learning something that had to hurt before it could feel better.

I called Judith and I asked her to please come get me. I told her I was suicidal and didn't want to be alone right now, that I needed to be with someone. She came and got me and took me back to the trailer. I just wanted to regroup and try to relax, but then she flipped out on me and started screaming at me to do her dishes. She said, "That I shouldn't sit around and be lazy and feel sorry for myself." That if I was going to stay out there with her for the night that I would have to do some work because I couldn't just sit there and do nothing, "She wasn't going to tolerate that," she said.

I was crying terribly at this point. This woman had waited until I was at her trailer in Waterford, about 15 miles outside of Erie where my home with Isaac was, to lash out on me during a time that I was mentally and physically exhausted. I didn't drive. I didn't have a car so that I could leave on will. I was stuck there.

I remember telling her, "I'm about to kill myself and all you care about is me doing your dishes so that I can earn my keep for staying here tonight?" She would yell again, "What you want me to do, feel sorry for you?" I said, "No, I just need some support right now."

I'm saying all of this while staring out the trailer window and doing her dishes. She would not stop screaming at me until I did her dishes.

That night I would bleed some more. I had also developed an ulcer due to all the stress which made it very difficult to eat or even drink water. When I went into the emergency room again that morning, I would find this out as well.

I spoke to my doctor who had known me for many years by now. He told me that the way things were going that I should expect to miscarriage. I was only about 4 weeks along.

I entered my relationship with Kevin at a very young age. I was growing up and my ideas on relationships were maturing. Again perhaps I never faced the fact that my parent's relationship was unhealthy. And until I admitted that fully to myself, I would base my relationships on the principles I saw. I knew in my heart they weren't right, but I had nothing to compare my intuitions with. I kept to myself at this time a lot. Nolan, the man I met before would resurface into my life. He would be a breath of fresh air for me during a difficult and confusing time.

I remember Nolan taking me to a waterfall overlooking the lake one night. He worked at this golf course so he knew this little overlook that was hidden from everyone. It was a full moon out that night and the water was lit up by the moonlight. He grabbed face in his hands and he said, "Does Kevin even tell you how beautiful you are?"

I remember thinking to myself, "No, he never dare tells me I look beautiful. He rarely compliments anything I do." Nolan would try kissing me, but I couldn't kiss him back. I was afraid to betray Kevin.

Nolan would come over and visit me. He didn't care how I looked. He didn't care that I was crying. He just wanted to come over and be with me. He didn't want to come over to have sex or take advantage of the situation. He just wanted to be with me to support me through this. I even remember one time him offering to try and get an apartment we could both live in. He was so sweet to me and I respected him so much. He was someone I never would forget.

Kevin would come over one time to bring over some old things I left. He walked in the door and went to go kiss me and I got close enough to him that I could smell another woman's vagina on his mustache. I never ever hit that man, but I swung my arm back as far as I could and landed into him. I was infuriated that he would have the nerve to come over to my place after he was lapping it up like a dog on some other woman.

I ended up losing the baby.

I would make one last visit to 130 Hill Rd. and that was to get my acoustic guitar that Judith gave me. I would leave behind everything else, paintings, cds, furniture, and high school yearbooks. I told Kevin this was it. I walked down those cement stairs and never looked back. He was crying. He was calling my name, and pleading with me, but I never ever looked back.

For now on, I would only look forward.

Chapter 7

keeping My Own Promise

My relationship with God would be even more personally pronounced. I wasn't ever into organization religion, but my faith in the spiritual world was prominent. Even though I was left alone all the time throughout my life, my spiritual guides never left my side. They loved me unconditionally the way I should have been loved by those physically present in my life.

There was a reason for the way my life evolved. There was a purpose behind every experience that had occurred up to this point. I may have not known at the time why, but I had faith and trusted what I was told. I also had to forgive myself and this was the hardest thing in the world to do, but I prayed about it every day and asked the universe to help me.

I felt like I was being given a second chance and I didn't want to waste any more time. When I handed myself over to someone that mistreated me, I wasted time and energy on something that was never intended to bare fruit. My relationship with Kevin paralleled my relationship with Judith. I kept trying to get love out of two people that were incapable of doing so. The words "I love you" are not enough. It is the action behind the person that gives away their true intentions.

Shame on them, but shame on me. I had kept going back trying to achieve different results and it didn't matter. The same behaviors would continue in their lives whether I was present or not. For my own health it was time to stand up and rise above the situation.

I stopped taking any of the blood pressure medicine. I stopped taking the migraine medicine. I stopped taking the ulcer medicine. I started to put the extra energy I used to put into other people and place it into myself. I continued to study and work hard. I think at this point I had about 7 different jobs. I would do illustrations for a local non-profit group, run sound at the Schuster Theater, work at the bakery, manage the college radio station, do my radio show with Shanna, write for a local entertainment magazine, and model for the mall there in Erie.

Plus I was still going to college full-time pushing a full credit load. I admit I had myself very busy, but perhaps I needed this at the time. The universe supplied me with opportunity and I met up with it through effort. I wanted to succeed more than ever. If you ever want to get back at the world or get back at someone do it through positivity, do it through drive. I wasn't going to sink to their level. I was going to rise above it.

But you know what is funny is nobody realized what I was accomplishing, only me. Kind words came more from strangers than people I knew, and so it would be for many years going forward. You don't go out and succeed to get accepted by people or to get a pat on the back. You go out to succeed to prove to yourself your own capabilities. You rise above the situation and make your own life, your own destiny.

Did I get harassed by peers and co-workers for striving so hard? Yes, every step of the way. There comes a time and point in your life where you have to trust your own instincts even if it goes against what everyone around you might be saying. You have to bypass the guilt and keep moving forward.

Come summertime, I took even more college credits. I even signed up for an internship at a commercial radio station and lucked out getting in with the Promotions Department. The 3rd day there, I got bumped up to work the morning show, a very high-rated time slot. I was working 60 hours a week at one point for the radio station and still managed the college station. The college radio station would be ranked #1 that year and even topped out the commercial radio stations for listener's choice.

The Communications Director at the university allowed me to manage the station for 3 months. The

Dean of the College wanted to shut the station down, but we begged for a chance to turn the station around and we did. The station even has a new home now and is a very prominent part of the college.

The universe had unfolded and changed my life in a miraculous way. Once you start to pay attention to life's guidance, you begin to see that your path in life is very well laid out, and that the lessons you learn today, prepare you for the path you will take tomorrow.

I loved radio. I snuck in personal development in our show, I talked about different lessons. Nothing drawn out or lecturing, but just little blurbs that would make people maybe pause and think. I was truly amazed by the response. People starting calling in and sharing their lives with us, it was very gratifying. I was about 20 years old now. It just warmed my heart on several occasions.

That Fall, Shanna and I graciously harassed the Communications Director to let us go to New York City for a college music festival. All our record label contacts were going to be there and a ton of bands. He secured the funds for us to go, so we took a train to the festival. We had a blast. I wound up meeting with one of the writer's for one of the major music television networks. The guy had asked me what I was going to do after college and I instantly blurted out, "I'm moving to New York City." He said, "Do you have a job lined up at all or anything?" "Nope, I said, but I will." He told me about a paid internship for a writer's position at their company. You better believe I had jumped on the opportunity and submitted my resume.

I put my resume on the back of two t-shirts and drew a caricature of myself on the front of the t-shirt on top of their company logo. I sent this off to both reviewers. They were very impressed. They had never been approached like that before. Isaac certainly didn't think that I would really be offered a job there. Or maybe he just didn't want to believe that it was possible.

Then one day when I came home from class, there was a message on my answering machine from the company. It was the Human Resource Department offering me a job in the writing department. It was a paid internship and the amount was higher than what I ever had been paid before. The only catch was the position was available right then.

I explained to them that I had 3 months left of college before I graduated. They explained, the deal was now or never. I cringed. I wanted the position so badly, but I worked so hard to get into college, and I was already right at the finish line. I would graduate and achieve my Bachelor's Degree in Communication Arts in a record time of 2.5 years instead of 4 years.

After much thought, I had to decline the offer.

I still planned on moving to New York City by myself after I graduated. I just felt that was where I needed to go, plus doors starting closing for me in Erie. I loved my job at the bakery as a cake decorator, but a new manager moved in and she did not like me at all. She started scheduling me in a different department and taking me away from what I loved, which was the cake decorating.

I didn't have a boyfriend either. I would date here and there, but nothing serious because I knew I would be leaving soon. I had the tremendous need to cleanse myself too. It was time to make more adjustments in my life. I cut all my hair off, made it real short. This made me realize who my true friends were and who was not. Needless to say, I didn't have too many friends.

I stopped doing so much volunteer work at the theater and the radio station. I dealt with my aloneness by writing songs. I would hang out on the stairwells and play my guitar and sing in the basement of the university. I had no idea the security guards would sit and listen to me all the time. I'm so glad I didn't know because I was always so paranoid of people hearing me.

I quit smoking again. Not exactly the smartest thing to do at the time of Final Exams and Thesis. My emotions were already gearing up and quitting smoking didn't help. Not to mention it isolated me from everyone even further, because so many people smoked in our college.

Shanna would soon decide to leave the show and leave our friendship in the process. She would write me a several page note speaking on behalf of her and others that knew me, on how I had changed, and no longer wanted to hang out with them, and that I was too focused. The letter hurt my feelings for sure, but now I could see the situation more clearly. I wasn't just getting ready to graduate college. I was getting ready to graduate this stage of my life. Whether or not it meant walking alone, did not matter to me. I was becoming more aware of my path and listening to what my own inner guidance was presenting me with.

I still did my show on Wednesday nights, but by myself now. One night a girl about 18 years old called me up and she told me that her boyfriend just broke up with her. She thought about killing herself. She turned the station on and I apparently said something that made her stop and think, and not do it. I was so touched that I asked her if she wanted to come down and do my show with me that night. She was so excited. She came down, and I put her on the air with me. She wound up having a blast. We sat there and talked in between songs. I never saw her again after that, but I was glad to see her walk away with a smile on her face and hope in her eyes.

I started wanting more meditation time, more time to myself. I was so involved, that I wasn't giving myself time to focus on my health and some priorities that I needed to address. So I started to minimize some of my commitments and responsibilities. I started saying, "No." Instead of "Yes, I'll do this" and "Yes, I'll do that." I started speaking up for myself and putting limitations on what I would do for other people.

Isaac would be distancing himself even further from me, especially once I actually got a job in New York City. On breaks from college, I would travel via bus to New York. One of my record label contacts put me in touch with an independent record label needing a manager. I made a trip and met with the owner and got the job. He wasted no time sending me out to represent the bands. I would head to New Orleans the day after I graduated college in May.

Everything was leading up to this transition. Isaac was mad at me and Judith I still hardly saw as she was engorged with her work. I felt miserable because I wanted to spend quality time with my family before I left and it was hardly that. I know Isaac was mad at me for leaving, but there was nothing left for me in Erie. Jobs in my field were scarce. I think maybe he was sad, but just didn't know how to show it.

I even got to see Beth's true colors towards me when I went out on a radio remote. Isaac was supposed to wake up to take me to the radio station about 5am, and Beth offered to do it last minute instead. She would sleep over the house a lot when they went out, so she was there.

On the way down the road she started lashing out on me. Told me how selfish I was and how Isaac does everything he can for me, and how inconsiderate I was. I didn't know what the hell she was talking about. I honestly never thought I asked for much. In fact I was very scared to ask for anything at all. I was just grateful to have a roof over my head and food.

I couldn't believe everything she was saying. I had no idea where this was coming from at all. I was crying hysterically, she just kept yelling the whole way there. I can't even remember everything she said to me, but I know it made me feel horrible.

I had a big morning too at the radio station. I had to be out in front of tons of people and I had to be on air and here I was getting yelled at only moments before. My life was always like that though, have someone reem you out and you gotta go on air or do a theater show, or work, or go to school. The show always went on. I would get myself together, clean my face up, and go out there and do what I set out to do.

Beth must have confessed what she did to Isaac when he got up because they both drove over to apologize while I was out with the radio station. I forgave her, but I never forgot about this hidden tension she apparently had for me.

My friend Susanne was proud of me. She was very supportive the whole time and so was another person that I wouldn't have expected, and that was a philosophy professor of mine in college. My philosophy professor was so touched with some of the philosophical papers that I wrote, that here she had saved them all this time, and gave them back to me. That was so sweet. I was shocked that someone understood my writing and actually encouraged it!

I had an English professor tell me I was the worst writer he ever met. He drilled everything I wrote no matter how hard I tried. I would never forget his criticism.

Also during this time, I wanted to prepare myself for the journey ahead so I made myself walk to school, which was miles away, instead of taking the bus. I made myself walk through the worst neighborhoods. People thought I was nuts. If someone stopped and asked me if I wanted a ride, I refused. I was on a walking meditation. I would be spiritually prepping myself the entire time.

Susanne always respected my intuitiveness. She was someone that didn't refute it like the others around me. In the first few years that we knew each other I picked up on something I would have no way of knowing about her. I would get a vision of her and another gentleman that I knew through Isaac, as having relations with one another. I told her about the vision and then she confessed in confidence.

Around this time, Susanne was leaving Al-Anon and exploring other spiritual venues, but we still kept in touch with one another through the transition. Al-Anon is very useful in providing families of alcoholics a safe place to share their strength and hope with one another, but it is not a permanent solution to discovering your life patterns with relationships. But it certainly helps peel back the layers of the onion in oneself.

I stopped finding going out with friends to be amusing. I was changing and getting my life in a new order. I didn't have all my nooks and crannies figured out just yet, but I was beginning to analyze these fragments of mine more closely. What did I like? What was my favorite color? I forgot these simple things because I was so caught up with the needs of the people I cared about.

The alcoholic was always the "center," the eye of the storm, and just as such, anything in its path would be disturbed by its fury. The closer you were, the more you would feel the effects. Somehow you would get sucked in and slowly taken down the path of destruction along with them. Even if your intentions were only to participate for a short period of time, it is easy to get wrapped up and entangled without even knowing.

I was along for the ride. Despite any flaws I had personally, I would stand by my mother. As life progressed and I met Kevin, I would continue the unhealthy relationship theme. However Kevin hit home. He had the alcoholic mother too, but he would carry on her alcoholism and I would refute mine.

Drinking or drugs was never more important to me than the people I cared about. I would drop it in a heartbeat, it meant nothing. It was nothing. All it was to me was something to occupy your hands and mind. Now I am not going to say I didn't drink or experiment because I sure did, but it didn't entertain me as much as it would others.

I was more fascinated with trying to "discover" what the big deal was. How could people abandon everything for something not even concrete? Just as they were addicted to alcohol and drugs, I was addicted to seeking out these unhealthy links to others only because I was accustomed to the tormented lifestyle, and thought that was the only way to live.

I somewhere along the way lost my sense of self worth which is kind of comical because I had no reason to feel unworthy. I was active. I modeled. I was creative and was able to accomplish almost anything I set my mind to. But that hole existed and would continue to exist for years after removing myself from my family. It became my mission to rebuild and recreate my own guidelines in life.

I was in a transition state now. I began to realize that nothing was stable and that everything around me was on unstable ground. My family relationships were that of association. I had no strong ties, no strong foundation that would make me stay there in Erie. Coming close to the end of my college career, I would be reminded more and more of that reality. The universe has a way of closing one door and opening another. It was like magic. My old state of affairs was no longer comfortable. Friends didn't want to hang around me. Family dealt with my leaving by limiting time spent with me. It was interesting how different people started treating me.

When I speak of doors opening and closing, the same occurs with people. When we have someone we care for walk out of our lives for whatever reason, the universe replaces them with someone else, however we don't always know it was planned that way. After Kevin and my other friends kind of dissipated, I had a friend that I made named Stephen. He was a great confidant. He had a stable job and family life. He had a good relationship with his parents and siblings. He was a caring guy. I never had any sexual relationship with him. It was only based on care and friendship.

He had respect for me and I had respect for him. It was so important to me to have these types of relationships with a male not having any hidden agenda with me. He was like a best friend to me at the time. He wanted to do things for me. He wanted to go take trips or just have fun together. I had really enjoyed his companionship.

I felt so comfortable around him that I even eventually would sing and play my guitar for him, which was a huge step for me. Before I would leave, even that friendship would take a turn. He wrote me a long letter. He ended up wanting to be more than just friends, but I couldn't do that. Something just kept telling me to go, to leave Erie.

So anything or anyone that may have opted to have me stay there, it just wasn't going to work. It was the insides of me telling me I needed to go now. I needed to see that there was another way. I needed to build my own life based on new principles and new surroundings.

The universe, my spiritual guides, and God were sending me messages more frequently that I was on the right path. I started meditating even more and spending a lot of time focusing myself to build strength for the journey I was about to embark on.

One of the last nights spent with Stephen, I would get a dream/vision. I would always get these periodically in my life. My dreams would show me reality or guide me as to where I should be. This dream was different. God was telling me something directly. What would I see? I only saw light and heard the voice speak to me. I was told, "I'm going to have you say this out loud." I said, "Why?" The voice said, "Because I know you will forget what I said, so you will say it out loud and your friend will hear, and remind you of my words." At that point, I laughed at how well they knew me.

Sure enough the next morning I would awake and Stephen asked me, "What were you dreaming of this morning?" I said, "Why do you ask?" He said, "Because you started laughing and then just said, "Keeper of the Light." That was it. That was my message. Then I remembered what I was told and the conversation I had.

I didn't know the meaning as of yet, but those words would stay with me.

Chapter 8

New York City

In life, there will always be a catalyst to carry you or get you to where you need to go. It may not be a permanent solution, but it will nonetheless be a stepping stone for you to step out of one stage of your life and into another. The timing will be perfect.

The week of graduation was difficult. I had quit smoking several weeks before as a part of my preparation and commitment. I had a lot on my mind though. My own mother was so engaged with her work that she told me she didn't even know if she could make my graduation ceremony. Then she asked me, "What is your major again?" She would ask me that a couple of times before I left.

She had no idea how important this was to me. She didn't even no what I was studying for the last couple of years. I let her know about my graduation ceremony months in advance so she could plan to take off. She even said she was going to throw me a big graduation party. So nobody else made arrangements for me because Judith said she would handle it.

At the last minute, nothing was done. She told everyone, even her own family, that she just didn't know if she could make it. No party was planned. I was just crushed, not about the party, but about the fact that I would graduate college, and my own mother wasn't even going to be there.

I had to give my Thesis presentation that week too before the graduation day. I would go in front of 3 panelists, all professors of mine. I would wind up losing concentration and hardly being able to defend my own argument in my thesis. My mind was elsewhere. I was so disappointed in myself.

I made it through and actually got a "C" on the thesis which was low for me. I went off to the restroom nearby and just started crying. It wasn't about the thesis. It wasn't about leaving. It was about the one person in my life that I would always try to get to notice me and always try to get to want to know me. It was about my mother.

Days before graduation, Judith's sisters, Jeanie and Peggy would approach Judith about attending my graduation. Jeanie told her, "Judith, this graduation is only going to happen once. You do whatever you have to do to make sure you are off to be there." The sister that had sexually experimented with me when I was little, actually is the one that went out and bought cake and balloons to throw me a party at my grandparents house. Talk about weird, but I was grateful nonetheless, extremely grateful.

Everyone got together at the last minute to throw me a little party after my graduation. I went though the ceremony, Isaac and Beth were there, my Grandma, Jeanie, Peggy, and I think a few of my cousins showed. Judith showed up last, but at least she showed.

My party raised me $300 dollars to take with me to New York. I was very grateful for everyone's generosity.

I was set to leave for New Orleans for a record label conference right after I graduated college, only days after. I wasted no time and the universe wanted it that way. Everything happened so quickly, that I was swooped out of Erie without a moment to look back.

After New Orleans, I came back to Erie and got ready to leave for New York City. I would take a greyhound bus to get there. I always loved taking the bus as it just gave me the time I needed to separate myself from all that just went on. It gave me the quiet time that I needed to just think.

My new boss would pick me up from the Port Authority in downtown New York City. I started work days after. I was in charge of going out and attending shows, getting promotional flyers printed up, distributed, and sent out, and scouting out new bands for the label.

But money would not be coming in enough for me to count on. After a couple of weeks of work, I was paid $400. I was living where I worked for the time being until I could get on my feet, but I eventually had to get another job on top of working for the record label.

I went to the temp agencies there and landed my first assignment the next day. If anyone ever wanted to accuse me of anything, I will be the first to admit at that time in my life, I was not a very well polished woman. I never wore dress suits or office garments and you never saw me in a pair of khakis. My clothes were artistic to say the least.

The only time I wore fancy dresses and business attire was if I was modeling those clothes for a company. So I showed up in a pair of Doc Martins which are like fancy combat boots really, a long black skirt, and a light blue dress shirt with a backpack.

I remember the temp agent asking if I had high heels to wear, I can remember just laughing. I would wind up getting several jobs there though and soon left the record label. It was actually perfect timing too, Susanne my confidant, had a daughter that actually lived in NYC at the time. She came up to visit her daughter at the same time that I was finding out that I wanted to leave the record label, so her daughter gave me a place to stay in the interim period. I would find an apartment close by to her with a roommate. I found the roommate through an agency there. I paid $600 for a room in a two bedroom apartment.

Every thing job wise was going great. I was able to make $14 to $15 and hour, but nothing was stable. I never knew where I would be from one week to the next. I re-approached the major music television network that I was offered a position with now that I was in New York. They would call back, but my roommate would never give me that message.

I actually heard the message from the HR person on the answering machine by accident one time and that's how I found out. I would find out a week late that they were again interested in me working for them.

One night soon after, my roommate snuck into my bed and I awoke to his hands around my neck. I would be hovered over by a naked man for over 12 hours. I eventually pretended that I was asleep. He would check me though and get right in my face, but I wouldn't move. He started freaking out, throwing dishes everywhere on the floor, I stayed still and never moved. Eventually he left the apartment. I grabbed what I could of my belongings and shoved them in my backpack and left.

I would call a Jewish guy I met weeks ago and he would let me stay at his place for a few hours. He eventually came with me to go back and grab whatever personal items I could carry. When he went back with me, the roommate was naked in his bed, passed out. He never moved. I left the brand new bed I bought and any little furnishings. I grabbed some of my clothes and my guitar and that was it.

I didn't know what to do. Susanne's daughter was gone for the week so I couldn't stay there. I just shelled out $1200 for my security deposit and rent. I had no money to find another place. I even tried staying at the YMCA, but they were full. So I had to do the only thing I could do and hop back on a bus to Erie.

I was disappointed because now I had no idea what was before me. I thought I knew what I was going to do and where I was going to be, but I didn't. I had moved to New York City and stayed there for only 3 months.

I had a taste of "something" and within those 3 months I would learn even more than what a school could teach. I learned a little more about what there was and what I was not. I got to taste what I thought I would be involved with from here on out, the radio and music industry. I found out that it truly didn't satisfy the person I would become only years later.

I always enjoyed helping people. I did a lot of community service stemming back from middle school. No matter what was going on in my life or what phase of teenage years I was going through, I always enjoyed volunteer work. It made me forget about myself and focus on others that were less fortunate or in need. You can put your own life into perspective when you see that you could actually have it worse off.

The choir I was involved in would go and sing at the old Soldiers and Sailors Home. I remember begging one organization in college to let me help them at their Thanksgiving Dinner for the homeless. I would get so touched that it would just bring tears to my eyes. Just watching people be illuminated with gratitude over the smallest of items just touched me beyond measure.

Even when I was in New York, I met a girl who was handicapped that would always pass out flyers at the shows I went to. I always enjoyed her. I would even go help her pass out flyers after I got off of work. We would go to shows too. She was so sweet and perhaps misunderstood because of her appearance, but she was brilliant. I was supposed to go see her that day I came back to Erie, I felt terrible that I missed her. I called and explained what happened and I just remember her saying she was going to miss me and that I was her friend.

You learn in life to compare your moments. The moments that made you feel good and the moments that made you feel not so good. Then you do what you can in your life to allow good moments have more of an opportunity.

I wasn't after money. I never was. I have been offered some very high salaries, but refused them. It wasn't about the dollar. It was about waking up every morning and knowing that I did something that would make a difference in my life or in the lives around me. That was what drove me. That is what gave me strength to get up instead of staying down.

However my strength was also my weakness. I wanted to live a spiritually justified and giving life, but

I had to also accept that I live in a material world. It would be a balance I would fight with for many years.

Chapter 9

Back to Erie

Now that I knew what life was like outside of Erie, it was very difficult to be back. Granted I was glad I got away from New York with my life, but it was hard to be back in Erie just the same. I was determined to get back to New York, but the reality was, the universe wanted me to sit tight. There was something else in store for me, but I certainly wasn't aware of it.

I got to see who my friends really were though when I left, because hardly anybody called me or wrote at all. I had my philosophy professor keep in touch, which was always so encouraging and Susanne, but other than that, if I didn't call old friends, they didn't call me.

So now that I was back I kept all of this in mind with people that were my "friends." Nothing had changed either. People were doing the exact same things they did when I left. Everyone migrated to the bar with the drink specials for the night. I participated in that group for a little while, but after two weeks, I was wondering what the point was.

I was of drinking age, but I just wasn't very in to drinking. I drank even less now that I was legally able to. Isaac always tried encouraging me to go out to the bars too, which I did to appease him, but I just eventually couldn't do it. I guess he just didn't want to see me staying home on Friday nights.

I had a terrible time finding work. Now that I had a college degree, it seemed like I couldn't find any work in my field. I was very antsy. I had started smoking again to somehow pacify my nerves and my own indecision. Judith was very encouraging, she told me I could make good money if I started working at McDonalds and worked towards being a manager,

"They have great benefits," she would say. "What was your major in college again?" I just sighed to myself.

Eventually I asked for my old cake decorating job back. It would keep me busy while I searched for other life options. I couldn't stay in Erie, the mere thought was so depressing to me I couldn't stand it. It was a constant reminder and feeling of just never quite fitting in. I was raised here, but I didn't feel at home.

I did get my old cake decorator job back. People treated me a little different when I came back. Maybe they felt like I betrayed them when I left, I never knew really. People wouldn't talk to me as much and the new female manager that didn't like me very well before, started scheduling me more and more in the bread department away from decorating.

On days off I would spend my time trying to send out resumes at the career center at my university. I came across something that was extremely exciting to me. It was a nationwide volunteer program. This just caught my eye. I immediately inquired about signing up. They would send you to a location and you would work there for just a living expense stipend.

At the time there was a program that was seeking a volunteer in 3 places, Rochester, NY, Gilroy, CA, and Tulsa, OK. I got accepted to the position in California. It would take a month before they actually went ahead and said yes though. I had been back in Erie for two months already and I was just aching to do something. So the beginning of October 1997 I would still be working at the bakery. They would not notify me of whether or not I was accepted until later. So everything was up in the air.

I again was trying to get my mother to spend time with me. She always had an issue of doing something with me one-on-one. She always had to involve other people which made me feel like she was more or less parading me around than spending time with me. Kind of like, "look I'm a mother, look everyone, I'm spending time with my daughter."

On a whim she asked me if I wanted to go camping with her down in Cooks Forrest for the AA Convention they have in the Fall. I jumped on the invitation. We were going to spend the whole weekend together. She just bought a new dog. She was all excited about him. Everything revolved around the dog. Judith had that way about her. She was like a little kid literally with a short attention span. One minute obsessing about one thing and forgetting about something else the next minute.

She always loved animals but was weird with them. When I was little I would come home and my cat would be gone or one of our animals would be put to sleep. Quite terrible when I think of this now as an adult, but that was her behavior with them.

So she wanted to take her dog with us camping, but the place we were going to stay at didn't allow pets. She knew that in advance, but she still insisted on taking him. So we finally get on the road and head about an hour and a half to two hours away. And then once we get there and set up the tent, she says, "I better take Brutus back home and then I'll come back."

I tried to convince her to stay, then I was like okay I'll watch our stuff and you go drop the dog off. Luckily one of her old AA buddies was right beside of us named Scottie. He was a wild looking guy, I think in his 40's. He hung out with me while I waited for my Mom. Mind you I had no money with me and no car. I can't even remember how I got food that night. I think other people around let me snack off what they had. She left me with cigarettes, a tent, and the odds and ends we brought to camp.

Scottie kept telling me, "Your Mom will be back." I would tell him, "She's not coming back tonight." Something in me just told me that she wasn't going to come back. Cell phones weren't popular yet, so had no way of getting a hold of her either. Sure enough she never came back that night, or even that morning. Scottie and I walked up to Serenity Rock and I saw a hawk. I told Scottie, "She's here now, let's go back to the camp." He said, "How do you know?" I said, "Because I just got my message."

She came back, but she was not going to stay. She offered to take me to get a few groceries. After that, she was gone again. Scottie said, "How is she leaving her young daughter out camping by herself?" That's how she was. She could never handle one on one time. She was paranoid too. She had been away from the program and not dealt with her own shit so being there was hitting a little too close to home. I knew that's what it was really about.

I always gave her opportunity and each time she would fail miserably to prove herself. I always gave her the benefit of the doubt because she was my mother.

That Sunday she came back and we packed everything up. Back to work I would go. I felt like I was in the middle of the road. Erie was no longer feeling good to me nor was it ever and I didn't know if the opportunities I applied myself to would bare any fruit. I was disappointed in my trip with Judith, but it was peaceful without her there. Her energy was very imbalanced. She was very insecure and uneasy with herself.

I never wanted her to feel bad. I never wanted her to feel bad about herself. When she came back, I didn't start yelling at her or freaking out. I talked to her and told her it wasn't right to have handled it that way. I was 'her' daughter, and I trusted that she was going to come back, but I told her, "I knew you were going to leave me there."

I think back to that now and wonder how she could sleep that night knowing that she left her daughter in the woods. I honestly couldn't do that, I would be worried sick. Every hour would seem like a day. That was always the difference between her and me. I cared a lot. I stood by my word unless some emergency prevented me from it. I looked people in the eyes when I spoke to them. If you asked for my word it was an honest one.

So much for spending quality time with my mother. Work at the bakery would become even more hilarious. One day when the manager stuck me in the bread department again so I could stock shelves, I waited on an older man. He paused for a moment and looked me right in the eyes. He told me, "You have something very special in your eyes that you don't see in everyone." He was probably over 75 years old, but I needed to hear what he said. He told me that and just walked away. I knew what he meant though and I needed his message.

He saw in my eyes the truth. I was surrounded by people that never saw my truth nor wanted to. They looked at me and looked right through me. I had people around me for all my life and not one of them saw in my eyes what this stranger saw in me now.

I would find out soon that I was accepted to the volunteer program out in California. By October 31, 2007 I would be sent to Washington, D.C. for training and briefing.

When I came back to Erie, I would start packing up my belongings. I asked the headquarters if I could take a train to Gilroy instead of flying and they granted my request. I told them, "If I'm going across country, I want to be able to see it."

I was so excited. Isaac I think was disappointed in me. He wasn't dealing well with me leaving, so I guess he tried not to deal with it at all. I didn't want it to be that way, but I couldn't control the situation either. There was a reason for all of this.

Isaac dropped me off at the train station, made sure I got my ticket and left. It was kind of a cold goodbye, but symbolic all at the same time. I would be at a cold train station by myself with just a backpack at 3:30 in the morning.

I sent out some boxes to the apartment I would be staying at in Morgan Hill, CA. I didn't want to lug anything with me. I had just a backpack with a change of clothes, my wallet, a couple cans of black beans and vegetables, and a can opener. I hardly ate a lot. There were a lot of emotions running through me. I was embarking on this huge change, but it was not just about a change of place. It was about physically distancing myself from the life I had grown to know. I would now travel 2100 miles away.

The journey there was amazing. I met a lot of different people along the way. I just stared out the windows in amazement. I remember that first night on the train there was a little boy behind me and his mother. He was crying. I loved the mother's response to him. She just held him and kept saying over and over, "I love you, I love you." I was amazed. That was what it should be like. A mother loves unconditionally. This was one of my lessons along the way, to see how other people love, and to see how other people live.

I would arrive days later at the train station in Salinas, CA where Corina and her two daughters would meet me. They had no idea what I looked like and nor did I have any idea what they looked like. So when I got there they had a sign outside with my name on it.

I stepped off that train and I saw such a warm loving smile greeting me. She was my supervisor for the company that I would be working for, a local housing authority in Gilroy. She gave me a hug right away. She was a little shorter than me, had long dark hair and wore glasses. She was a Mexican woman. Her daughters were so cute. They had dark hair too and dark complexions.

Me on the other hand, I was white girl, and a pale white girl at that. I had no idea that I was going to be working in a place where I was the complete minority. I thought that was hilarious. My adventure soon began.

Chapter 10

Gilroy, California

L ife has a weird way of getting you where you need to be at just the right time. It seemed that now, the further I was away from the chaos of my family, the closer I was able to get to my intuition and myself. After Corina and her girls picked me up from the station, she said, "You must be hungry, let me pick up some food for you." I was so timid about people buying me anything. After all, I was so used to people making a big deal out of anything "little" that they did for you, that I was extremely and unusually grateful for someone's generosity towards me.

So Corina bought me a meal at the Jack n' the Box and I was so impressed. I know that sounds silly, but I wasn't used to people being 'nice' to me or being 'sincere.' Back at home there was always a penalty or hidden agenda along the way. It's when someone does a kind act without even thinking twice about it that I admired so much.

Corina would then take me to the activity center, the other project I would be working for. This center was very exciting to me because it was artistic and creative. They had an opening night there. I had my first smoothie made with tofu. I always liked tofu, but never was around others that shared this liking so I was excited. I met everyone there and they were all so welcoming.

That night I would be taken to my new apartment. It was a studio apartment in Morgan Hill, CA about 10 minutes outside of Gilroy. It was perfect, because there was a bus that would take me straight to the housing authority, only blocks away.

I forgot to mention that during the time that I moved to California, El Nino storm was there so we had an unusual amount of rainfall and flooding. Being from the East Coast, I was not used to this.

That night I had a vision of a dark haired man bringing me my mail. It was kind of a vision that told me to pay attention to this person I would meet. The next day, I had a dark haired man come to my door. When I first was given the address of my apartment, they gave me a different apartment number than what they put me in, so all my mail went to this 'dark haired man' instead of to me.

So low and behold this would be how I met Diego. He was a nervous man about in his 30's with very short dark hair with a balding spot beginning in the back that you couldn't see unless you took off his hat. He had a young face though and a light complexion which surprised me from his Mexican background. Our encounter would be the beginning of a very important friendship in my life.

I knew my monthly stipend would not be a lot of money as I was doing volunteer work there at both housing authority and the activity center. I would receive $550 a month. My rent was $50 so I had $500 to spend on food and my transportation to and from the office.

I would meet my volunteer partner that I was first introduced to in Washington, D.C.. His name was Ethan. He was going through an interesting life transition soon after the project began, so the timing was perfect.

Like with any project that I take on, I hit the ground running. I was ready to get started right away, but the universe had others plans. Nobody knew what to do with us two volunteers. We started fixing computers around the office and working with the IT Manager there, but we were supposed to build a website for housing facilities. And nobody knew exactly how to instruct us.

They never had government volunteers on site before either so poor Corina was very new to the responsibility. About a month or so into the project, we were not much further along. No matter how much I pushed for us to be, we were still stuck at square one.

My partner Ethan would soon experience a break up from his long term relationship and engagement which would send him into a deep life assessment.

This occurred in early December, so about two weeks before Christmas, I saw an advertisement for the greyhound bus, where if you buy one ticket, your friend rides for free. I was going to try and go to Erie for Christmas and a bus was all I could afford to take, so I asked Ethan if he wanted to come with me.

He was very excited. He had never ventured out of Gilroy. So we traveled to Erie and back to Gilroy. We got close to one another after his breakup. We had a special bond during his life transition. He was discovering a whole new world and became more willing to live outwardly, but he would have a lot more discovering of himself to do.

Ethan left the project in January and now it was just me left with this huge task at hand. I kept it together though. I wasn't going to give up. In the meanwhile, the past couple of months I had started getting into art. Emotions began coming out of me like never before. I didn't have anything in my apartment except for bare necessities and whatever anyone donated to me from the office there. They took up a wish list for me and everyone donated something to me to help out. It was so sweet. I wasn't used to this kindness. Sure I got hand-me-downs when I was younger many of times, but that was from people that knew me. Here were people that had no idea who I was and they were willing to help me.

Someone donated a television to me, but it only had one channel, and it was Spanish, so watching television was out of the question. So I bought some cheap watercolors, tore up a sponge I had, and pieced together several sheets of paper so I could draw on it with a Sharpie Marker.

The next day or so, Diego saw my drawing and was impressed. He offered to buy me a real watercolor tablet. I was honored. We went to a local art store and he bought me my first watercolor tablet. I got a set of watercolors and some more Supersized Sharpie Markers.

With work being sporadic, I had a lot of alone time on my hands. Something was happening inside of me. A transformation that needed to take place finally was happening whether I wanted it to or not.

I always kept myself busy before. I kept active almost to the point of exhaustion. Perhaps that was necessary for the time and place, but now was different. Life was slowing down for me so I could actually stop and look at it.

I could write now, I could really write. Nobody could interfere anymore. Nobody would hunt for my journals and read everything I wrote to interrogate me about it. I could be real. As I would write about the reality of my life it was like I saw myself for the first time. Not just me, but what people I was surrounded with before. I took off my blinders and I looked.

I went back and fourth from my journal to my watercolor pad. I would write about my feelings and recall a certain point in my life and then hash out my emotions on paper. There was nobody to hide from anymore. Once my body and my mind realized this, it was like it started purging all it could. I prayed a lot. I meditated a lot. I sang and played my guitar a lot too. Nobody was there to tell me not to.

Admitting my own wrong doings or faults in life also made me look at others involvements and roles. There were times when I was too hard on myself. There were times that I didn't give myself the credit I deserved. I placed a lot of blame on myself for things other people did to me. There were times when I disrespected myself.

I finally was looking at the people I had distanced myself from. I was looking at my life. I was far away, had very little belongings, and little money, or material items, and I had more than I ever had. My headaches were occurring less. I wasn't getting sick as often.

Every day, I would just do the same therapy at night, write, meditate, and then just sit over a blank tablet crying over my realizations and drawing. My room became a virtual gallery. I had paintings hanging everywhere. I never was an artist. I had so much trouble evening saying the word 'artist' in reference to myself.

Every day, Diego would come home from work and want to see the new painting. I was terribly shy about it, but I would always show him. I made a promise to God, and to myself, that if someone asked me to share a talent, whether it was my art, or singing, that I would no longer hide from it. I had a commitment to keep. Abilities are not given to us for our own amusement, they are given to us to benefit and contribute to those around us.

I had also started talking with Diego, after all we lived right across the hall from one another. He was great because he asked questions. I never had someone ask me about me, ask about why I thought the way I did. All these people I knew before, they just never pushed past that level. Granted I had a few girlfriends and guy friends that I shared personal tidbits with here and there, but to actually have someone ask me about my spirituality and family was very interesting.

Diego was raised in a Christian home. He had two parents, no divorce, and a sister. His Mom and Dad were so sweet and caring. She was always cooking something every time we went over there. They were very giving people.

Once Diego got to know a little more about me and my background he asked me once, "Mija, (means my little one in Spanish), "Why do you believe in God?" If there is anyone I ever met that had an excuse to be mad at God, and to not believe in God, it would be you." He didn't understand, in fact this baffled him because here I was a non-church going woman, but spiritual. "Nobody made you believe in God, but yet you do." I had to smile at this.

I believed in God. I believed in this universal force that guides me constantly. My life, and the things that occurred in my life, were all merely preparation for what I was intended to be. I have no regrets and I would change nothing. Sure I had moments of great indecision, but I had trust and faith that there was a reason behind the occurrence. My faith was all I had. It was the only thing I could count on.

It is in a life of instability that I held on to the one thing that would keep me warm at night... my faith. I owned that faith. Nobody could break me from it. Nobody could tear it down.

Meanwhile at work, after Ethan left, I met with a housing developer named William to assist with the project. He was very honest with Washington on their goals. He told them that there was no way one person could perform what they were expecting me to perform. I was shocked, but was amazed by his honesty. He was right.

I had hung in there on the project this long, but finally made the decision to get out and start looking for other work. I found several temporary jobs that I worked randomly. I would also be put into contact with a Henna Tattoo Artist who would teach me how to do mendhi or henna tattoos. We started doing fairs together.

Diego had taken still images of my art and made a website page for me. It would be the very first time my art would be up for the world to see. Then without me knowing, he submitted the link to the Public Relations Representative at Sanford Corporation. She would request an interview with me over the phone, and then forwarded me to another department to perform an interview there to discuss my art.

People were taking notice of my work and I was very surprised with this. I finally began to call myself an artist. It took a lot of practice, but I finally started to make myself say it.

I was still healing. I was starting to see why I had some of the relationships that I had with people. I understood the root of my own poor choices. The only way we can stop a life pattern from reoccurring in our lives over and over is to stop and realize what we are doing wrong, realize what choices we are making, and then work towards change and healthy alternatives.

I didn't have to be with alcoholics. I didn't have to smoke. I didn't have to be disrespected. It was time to put back all that was taken away. I was learning about myself and all the different layers that make me who I am. I was dissecting each layer and bringing up all the dirt to the surface.

This transition was not easy. It's hard to take a look at yourself. It's hard to even look at the people we have loved along with their truth, but it had to be done and California finally gave me a safe place to do it. The universe provided for me a safe place to detoxify my mind and regain my spiritual balance.

I had to spiritually cleanse myself as I was getting ready for the greatest moment of my life. I just had no idea the magnitude of the reward.

It was months after I left the volunteer program that it would be announced that they no longer needed an Apartment Manager for the building that I lived in, so I could no longer only pay $50 a month for my rent. I was going to have to find a place to move to soon.

I kept feeling called to Seattle, a place I never been to before. I was being told spiritually that my husband is there. I had no idea on how this intuition would transpire into reality. I had no idea what would get me to Seattle.

I would wind up going to a party and meeting a girl named Julie. We would exchange phone numbers and wind up talking to one another. She told me she was supposed to take this trip up to Seattle, WA with her boyfriend, but they just broke up. I told her I was just thinking of going there. So I wound up going there with her for the weekend. I loved it and got an apartment there days later at the Granada Apartments. I would move there the end of July of 1998.

Before I moved to Seattle I was going to go to France to visit a pen-pal that I had kept in contact with over several years. I even bought my ticket months prior, but found out that Judith and Brock were going to get married July 4th. Judith knew I couldn't be there.

I felt terrible about not going, so I bought a ticket to fly to Erie to make sure I was there. I never did go to France and lost the money I spent on the ticket, but I felt Judith was more of a priority. I wanted to support this new sober marriage of hers.

I never told Judith I was flying in. I didn't tell anyone. I wanted it to be a surprise. I even bought a cell phone to have for the trip so I could call her and act like I was still in California. I showed up at her wedding minutes before the ceremony. I walked in to the room where she was at and she was just gathering her bridesmaids into a prayer circle before she went out to the ceremony. Her eyes were closed. I was shaking because I was so nervous and excited.

I went up and grabbed her hand and said the prayer with her and she opened her eyes and saw me. We both started crying. She looked so cute in her wedding dress. It meant so much to me to be there for her and share this special day with her.

I would stay for a week and then fly back to California to prepare for my move to Seattle.

Chapter 11

Seattle, Washington

D iego offered to move me to Seattle. He was terribly sad about seeing me go, but he knew I just felt a calling to go there so he respected that. I would continue to do art full time in Seattle. I had earned money from my henna tattoo shows that would support me for the month. I would fly back and fourth from Seattle to California once a month to do the shows.

I wasn't able to find temp work in Seattle for some reason, I guess the universe wanted me to keep preparing myself and learning this new trade. I began taking better care of myself bit by bit. I kept painting. The more I painted, the better I felt. It was an amazing freedom for me. I felt like a tremendous weight had been taken off my shoulders.

I would stumble upon an intuitive reader named Michael. For some reason I just walked in and had him give me a reading. He helped validate this transition I had been having. He said to me something to the affect, "You need to know, you're not guilty. The place you came from, you don't need to go back to. That place carried a lot of hurt for you."

I knew exactly what he was talking about. He also warned me of a few people that I would encounter and a brief relationship I would have with a man. He also told me I wasn't going to be in Seattle for very long. I wasn't meant to be. This place was just a transition for me.

I went home and continued painting and playing my guitar. I always played and sang in the privacy of my apartment. There was a coffee shop outside, right across the street that I would go to just about every day. I did henna tattoos there for spare cash.

The owner of the coffee shop, Tim, would wind up letting me have an art show there. It would be my first exhibit. In the meantime, I would meet Alex, a tall, skinny guy with glasses. He was so fragile looking, but we started talking one night and just didn't stop. We hit it off immediately. He lived in a tiny one room place where you had to share a bathroom with the whole floor of residents. The first time I went over to his place, which was only houses up from me, his ex-wife happened to be stalking the building.

Not long after we started dating, I offered for him to move in with me which is very unlike me. After living with Kevin I had a lot of fears about ever being able to live with anyone again. But he moved in and this helped me recover from a lot of old fears I had. I was terrible about keeping groceries there for myself. My eating was so sporadic. So once Alex moved in, all of a sudden, I had groceries and full cabinets.

I started eating more meals. Alex was an old military man so he was more structured than I was. He ironed and folded his laundry very strategically. I was a wash n' go girl, but I was trying to be more 'feminine.' I still had a lot of rough edges. We got along great and living together wasn't as bad as I thought it would be except for Alex always had a sadness in him. He never was quite right with himself. He wasn't used to being loved or cared for at all, especially by women. He had several abusive relationships where he would get abused by the woman. He told me I was the best thing that ever happened to him. Even still, he never knew how to let someone love him, even me.

His lesson became my lesson.

I had walked around placing myself in relationships with men that would never bare fruit because I was so afraid of my own love being reciprocated. I was afraid of being loved. I didn't know what it was like. If I didn't learn this lesson I would only keep doing what Alex was doing, and that was being in love with my own pain. We lived together for about a month. I eventually found out he cheated on me.

He still needed to stay with me for about two weeks so he could find a place and I said that was fine. I ended up getting in touch with my old friend Stephen from Erie, but he was living in Raleigh, North Carolina. I told him what happened and he said he had enough frequent flyer miles to get me a ticket to come and visit. I jumped on the thought. So the day after Alex told me he was leaving, I was off on a plane to North Carolina.

I stayed there for about a week. I was pretty torn about the break up. Stephen said, "Wow I never seen you like this before." I wasn't all weepy or anything, but I was just bummed. I thought I was closer to "something" for a moment. I had that premonition about meeting my husband in Seattle, but maybe I was wrong.

Stephen noticed a change in me. I don't think he could ever really put his finger on what it was exactly, but he did notice. I began to notice too. I had a different self respect that I didn't have before. I didn't pretend I was all happy either. I let myself feel. If you constantly go around trying to protect yourself from being hurt, you also wind up preventing yourself from being loved. I didn't want to live like that anymore.

When Alex and I were together I had told him that the next place I would move to was going to be Atlanta, GA. He actually at one point was going to plan on moving with me. I never moved with anyone so it was a surprise. That was where I felt intuitively drawn to next and I had never been there either.

So I still continued on with my plans, but now I had even more motivation to do so. Alex broke it off with me in November. I would leave at the end of December from Seattle. I thanked Stephen so much for letting me stay with him. It had given me time to evaluate the situation and let life go where it needed to go.

The relationship we had was a very quick relationship, but I think it had a big impact on us both. I still spoke to Alex when I got back to Seattle. It was rather symbolic one night how we were preparing to part. I went to a show down at the Showbox with a couple of people I met, actually, Alex's friends. I walked home that night by myself at about 3AM. It was funny because there was a man up in front of me, sunken down with a very sad energy. Here it was Alex.

He had a couple more days left at my place before he would move out. So he slept on a futon in my living room. It was a bit awkward, but at least the majority of the time I was out-of-town.

I got very inspired to start getting serious about making the changes I wanted to make in myself. It was time to clean my act up and get serious. If I wanted a partner that didn't smoke then I needed to quit smoking. If I wanted someone that took care of themselves, then I needed to take care of myself. It was time to do good unto myself. I felt like I was running a marathon for some reason.

I finally quit smoking. I quit cold turkey. I am getting over a break up and decide to quit smoking, not the brightest of decisions, but I just used emotion and any extra energy I had towards accomplishing something. I made myself start running every time I wanted to smoke. I trimmed my body up and was finally living the way I deserved to.

I bought new clothes, completely different from what I normally bought. I started to polish the rough stone that I was. I started investing time into myself that I used to focus onto others.

I made plans to go to Erie and visit, and then fly to Atlanta to find myself an apartment before I moved. Why had I felt so compelled to go to Atlanta of all places? I have no idea, but it was embedded in me, and there were no doubt that was where I needed to be.

My trip back to Erie always through me off course slightly. I would always make appoint to go visit and spend time with everyone, especially around the holidays. This trip was rather hilarious though. It was a big ploy. I thought my Aunt Peggy and her Cousin Sandy and their spouses, etc. were taking me out to a bar just for fun. Then they call me down to their end of the table and start telling me that I should become a "waitress." They knew about me investing in my artwork and they gave me this big lecture about being a "waitress" in the meanwhile.

That was comparable to Judith telling me I should go work at McDonalds after I just graduated college. Not that I felt I was above anyone at all, because I have worked many jobs. No job is too small. I've scrubbed grungy toilets, cleaned public restrooms, and worked for a construction company even out in California. You do whatever you have to do to accomplish what you need to accomplish at the time.

But the mere fact that this "meeting" with me after they had a few drinks, to tell me what I should do with my life was a little far fetched for a 23-year-old-woman that had already traveled the country side and had been living on her own on and off since 17. Everyone thought I was crazy though for pursuing my art.

Before I left Seattle, the name for a domain name came to my head, and I wrote it down on a piece of paper in the last words of a sentence, "...because Silence Speaks"

That was it. That was what the name needed to be. So my art website became silencespeaks.com. Diego would design the site for me and I would end up teaching myself web design from here on out to maintain and redesign it later on.

I found an apartment down in Atlanta and I signed the lease. Then I flew back to Seattle, to finish up my art show and pack all my stuff up. As usual I got rid of a lot of things again. I would be saying my goodbyes to friends I made. I went to a café with a friend I met one night and I had to interrupt our meeting. I told him, "I'm sorry, but I have got to say something to this man over there."

There he was. I had seen him in passing so many times, but never said a word. Both men and women drooled over him at the coffee shop across from my apartment. He was so well presented that I never thought I would even be worthy enough to speak to him. His presence was strong. Everyone thought he was married or with someone.

For some reason, I had to go say something to him. So I went up to his table and sat down and blurted out, "Are you married?" He practically choked on his drink, and struggled to speak, and said, "No." I told him, "I'm sorry, I just had to ask that before I moved." He then asked me where I was moving to and I told him Atlanta, GA. He said, "That's funny, that's where my mom and brother live at." We talked a little longer, but it was still brief. I left the café and walked home.

A day or so before I was about to leave I would see him one more time and this was at the coffee shop. He was so serious looking, but then a little boy at the same time. Here he was playing pinball while he was doing his laundry. That was when we were officially introduced by a mutual acquaintance. His name was Richard.

He now knew that my art was hanging there at the café and he also knew that I left my business cards up by the register with my new address on them. I would leave the next morning for Atlanta and my new apartment.

Chapter 12

Atlanta, Georgia

T he night before I left Seattle, I started a very special painting. It would later be called "FaithsArrival." I worked on the painting diligently. It was a drawing of the cross that I received from the shippers that packed my guitar case when they shipped my belongings from Erie to California. The older man that picked up my boxes back then asked why I was moving to California, and I told him about me going out there to do volunteer work. As a kind sentiment he placed a cross necklace in a jewel box inside my guitar case.

The cross was silver but had a cloth emblem draped over it. I later on found the meaning that it represents that you will be protected while you do God's work. So I used this as one of my symbols in my painting.

The painting became a backdrop for a shrine that I was making for my husband. I had never in my life made a shrine of any sorts, but I felt completely compelled to do so. The desire was innate.

I gathered special cloth, gemstones, candles, and incense for my shrine. One candle would not be lit until he arrived and the other would burn every night for him while I was awaiting his arrival.

I spent many nights meditating around this shrine. I was preparing for something, but I had no idea of what it was, or who it was. In the meanwhile, I found a temp job that I worked during the day to keep me afloat financially while I worked different art shows in Atlanta.

In March, Judith and her other sister, Meredith, would end up driving down from Erie to visit me. This would be the first time any family members came to visit me while I lived out-of-state.

Judith had finally quit smoking and was chewing her nicotine gum to help get her over her addiction. She had been smoking for well over 30 years at this time. The doctors found a lump in her throat that was considered cancerous so they removed it for her and urged her not to smoke again. So she took them serious and quit. I was very proud of her for this.

She stayed one night with me and it was nice. I had no furniture, only a computer and a single bed someone gave me from work recently. It was a nice visit, I actually enjoyed it. Nobody else was around so she was just herself with me. It was a pleasant change.

After she left, I would sit down to write a little letter on pink paper. It was a letter written to my companion, it was written on March 20th, 1999. I wrote: "Dear Companion, I know you are even closer to me now and soon we will be reunited. I long for your arrival and return to me."

I knew that he would be here soon, but I just had no idea exactly who, or exactly when. I was amazed at

what was being written from me too. I knew this man.
I knew him from before in another time, but I didn't
have all the pieces to this puzzle yet. Atlanta was a
weird place, not the greatest of places for a non-driver
to live either. The energy was very odd there and I
never felt quite at home, but I was there for some
reason.

A week later, I would find out what that reason
was. I received a phone call from Richard, the man I
approached before I left Seattle. He was in Atlanta
visiting with his Mom and brother helping them move.
I offered for him to come over and visit and he said that
would be great. I think he had to take two different
cabs to get to me that night, but he finally arrived.

When he first walked into my apartment, he
immediately noticed the shrine in the corner of my
living room. He saw the pink letter under the candle. I
don't know how he saw it right away, but he did. He
told me, "That letter is for me."

My heart sank into my stomach, but I didn't say a word, I just smiled slightly. The whole time, I'm thinking to myself, "When my companion arrives, I will know, and he will get to read the letter. How did he notice the letter?"

We sat all night in my hardly furnished apartment and just talked. I'll never forget we were out on the balcony and he started telling me that he was just travelling around by himself. He was doing what I was doing, travelling on intuition, wherever he felt led to next, he would go.

He had moved to Seattle actually only a month after I moved there, but he came from Florida. We lived only a block away from one another in Seattle and never realized it. We were learning more and more about one another.

Then finally, while he was sitting in my office chair and I was sitting close to my shrine, he said, "I need to tell you why I really came to Atlanta." I was listening so intently. "I didn't just come here to visit my family, I came here for you." "I know this sounds crazy, but I was told you were my wife." There were long pauses in between his words, but I listened intently.

If I had to walk through fire to get to this moment in my life, I would. I was in such awe, that no words could come from my lips only tears of joy. He continued to tell me that a week ago, a day prior to me writing my letter to my companion, something told him to "Go, now." He left his job, his furniture, and any large personal items all behind and he hopped on a red-eye flight that night with a suitcase of clothes.

The whole time we were in Seattle, his spirit guides would tell him, "There is your wife," but he never could speak to me, he couldn't bring himself to do it. He would be told this over and over. Then finally after I had already left Seattle, that inner voice was telling him that he had to go now and get his wife, and he did.

He told me the story and again, I could say nothing, I was in shock. The only thing I could do was reach down and grab my pink letter and hand it to him. He was the owner, no one else. I lit the candle that I promised to light once I knew my companion had arrived. I knew now, he was before me.

Chapter 13

Our Lives Before

I had moments in my life where I had recalled memories from a different time and place then the life I live in now. I had no one to share these moments of recollection with though as certain people in this world would pass this off as insanity more than recollection.

The first night I spent with my husband, my memories were becoming severely more pronounced. I remembered him. I remembered his lips. I had flashes and visions appear to me all at once. My long lost love, how he was present before me once again. I was overwhelmed with tears I was too hesitant to explain. I didn't want to scare him away. If I told him, would he think that I was crazy?

I also had a horrible time saying his name, "Richard." That was not his name to me. It made me cringe every time I tried to say it. I ended up calling him my "precious." I couldn't bear to use that name of his. It was because I knew his face by another name, but I could not recall the name.

I finally got the courage to tell him what I was seeing and feeling and here he felt it too. He could not bear to call me "Heather." He called me his "wife" instead. We started recollecting our past. We even had unfinished business that we had to deal with.

Days after our reuniting, we had broken out into a disagreement. It was the strangest disagreement I ever had because it had nothing to do with this life at all. It all dealt with our past and how we were separated before, and the dark haired man that couldn't stand to see us together. I thought my love was dead, that was what they told me.

After we sat there and explained both of our sides of the story, that was it, we were able to move on and live our lives now in the present day. We had a lot of catching up to do. Meanwhile, other spiritual occurrences were going on. It was rather odd. It was like we made "something" quite disturbed over our reuniting.

I had always burned a candle in my bedroom. There were even nights where I let it burn all night. It was far away from the bed. One night when my husband and I were in the bed together, we looked down and saw half of the bed spread caught on fire.

The candle was too far away from the bed to have caught it on fire. My husband grabbed the comforter and smothered the fire out. We would then begin seeing other dark energies and round spheres appearing out of nowhere. I didn't know at the time what these were called, but later found out that these were orbs.

We had to get out of Atlanta soon that was growing quite apparent to us both. We were very adamant about getting our wedding bands right away.

It would protect us and link us together. In our previous lives we never had that and always wanted them so badly. For us the rings would symbolize our completion together.

We would buy two silver bands that very week.

How do you explain something like this to your family? My family knew of my intuition, but didn't pay attention to it. I think they more or less passed it off as coincidence if I had said anything intuitive. Half the people will pass you off as weird, but in their own private moments come to you on the side and say, "I've had this happen to me before…" "Or you know what, you were right about something."

I knew my entire story would sound out of proportion, but it was our truth. We would share our story on occasion with people who asked or people we felt comfortable with. They always walked away with goose bumps, because the truth has a way of making itself known.

I am sure it was quite odd for both of our families to find out about us. I never called him my boyfriend. We were never engaged. He was my husband from day one and I was his wife. There were absolutely no doubts in my head at all.

The first night I slept in his arms, I would finally rest, like I never had rested before. It was like I had been running all these years and finally I could stop and rest. I would live this life a thousand times over as long as I knew my reward was him.

He was such a polished man and I was so rough around my edges, trying to be more lady-like. I was trying to dress more appropriate and be neater. He ironed his clothes every day. He was spotless. I could get ready in 10 minutes. He would need an hour or two prepping time.

My husband would become the perfect compliment to my life. He would teach me how to take my time and enjoy my surroundings. He would appreciate all of me, the way no other would. Most importantly he would be intuitive. I could never discuss my visions, my intuitive messages with just anyone. Granted I met people along the way, but to be able and sit there one on one was something I truly embraced. Then to actually have him understand me and discuss his own intuitive occurrences was a true blessing. If you don't have someone to support you in the spiritual area of your life then you continue to hide in the sidelines with your thoughts and emotions.

I was never a bragger or one that liked being the center of attention. Granted almost everything I would do or succeed in led me to that stage, but it wasn't one that I intentionally placed upon myself. However, I soon accepted that your gifts from the universe are not yours alone, and to hide them, or hoard them would be to abuse the privilege you had been granted.

Having my husband by my side would give me the validation that I needed to face the truth about my family. Not only would he listen to me and my past family experiences, he would soon get to experience first hand what it was like.

Soon after we were reunited, I could no longer afford the apartment we were staying in. So we had to move in with my mother-in-law for a short while. We stayed there for about 3 months. I fell in love with his family. He had a mother and a brother. A small family, but a lot different from mine, I would learn those differences later on.

We ended up moving to Erie so that we could try to find work there. We both agreed before we even moved out of my apartment that we would get married in Colorado. So I guess it was the universe's way of having us get to Erie so that he could meet my side of the family prior to our marriage.

My husband would make the trip a definite learning experience for me simply by having his perspective alone and support. He would see things the way I saw them and validate my emotions during this time.

Chapter 14

Avon, Colorado

We stayed at the old house on June Street when we went to go visit Erie, PA. I would get a temp job at one of the major transportation companies there and work in the Public Relations Department under and executive named Susanne. Isaac and Beth still did not live together so Isaac let my husband and I stay with him while we were there.

We arrived in July, and then about late September my mother-in-law was diagnosed with cervical cancer. Mid-October she would have her surgery. My husband was beside himself. He took a bus back to Atlanta to be with her for her surgery and help take care of her afterwards. Meanwhile I stayed up in Erie to keep working.

About two weeks later he would come back to Erie and days later we would depart for Avon, Colorado. We both had jobs lined up there so we were ready to go. My mother-in-law would make it through the surgery and have a peaceful recovery. We were very grateful and at ease over this.

I think one of the greatest fears you have when something finally good happens to you is that the sky will fall out on top of you. You get so accustomed to insanity that once it stops, you are literally afraid of what may transpire to counteract the goodness.

Here we both were finally getting a "break" in our lives' of instability and we had no idea what stood before us. So finding out that my mother-in-law was in good health was just a tremendous joy. Cancer is certainly not something I would wish upon anyone, but in hind sight she was having a huge "stop" sign placed before her. She always was on the road driving a truck for many years, having cancer made her make the change she needed to go forward, and actually alter her career, and get off the road.

We departed for Colorado October 29, 1999. We were able to marry ourselves in Avon, Colorado on November 2, 1999. It was the greatest moment for both of us. He had originally taken my last name instead of me taking his last name. I wanted to keep my last name at the time because Isaac had no other offspring besides for me. The name would not be carried on. So I felt like I owed it to him to keep the last name.

As for my husband, his last name never meant anything to him because it wasn't even his father's last name. His mother had another child before she had him and she had asked his brother's father if she could use his last name and he allowed it. So my husband never identified with that last name and was ok with taking my last name. In fact, he always said when he was little, that he wanted to take his wife's last name. I had always said that if I ever was married that I would like my husband to take my last name.

Our stay was brief in Avon. We stayed there for about 5 months and then headed back to Atlanta, GA, but now officially as husband and wife. We later found out that Isaac and Beth were planning their wedding for June 30th and had asked us both if we would like to be in the bridal party. We agreed and ended up going back to Erie in May 2000.

We stayed in the old red house again on June Street. Every time we went back there, I would "see" a little more of myself and my life. I would realize how cold the house truly was. I would observe everyone around us through a different set of eyes.

When it came time for Isaac's wedding, I was proud to be able to share this moment with them. Isaac would move into Beth's house only a block away and put the old red house up for sale. It was a bitter sweet goodbye. Isaac had lived in that house for so long that I think it just secretly killed him to move from there. He loved his little house. He worked very hard to keep it and he was very sad to have left it.

My husband and I agreed to help fix the place up to help him sell it. He bought paint and we repainted the entire house. We cleaned it out and got rid of things that were there from when I was little.

One day I went to go write to my friend Susanne to let her know that I was having trouble finding work in Erie and so was my husband. I would wind up sending the email to the WRONG SUSANNE. I sent it to my old boss at the transportation company instead of my friend Susanne. I was so embarrassed terribly when I found out as the letter I wrote was lengthy and personal.

I apologized for my error. She wrote back and told me about a contract position over at the technology park, a new branch of the company. It would be a position I wound up filling for a whole year.

My mistake was not a mistake. Had I not sent the wrong email, I would have never known about the position because it wasn't even posted yet. I was very grateful to the universe for allowing me this opportunity.

It just killed my husband to not work. He had never had any trouble finding work until now. He always was financially comfortable and could basically do as he wished. Now the roles were reversed. He would embark on his own journey of finding his own niche.

For me the lesson was to actually have to stay at a job for longer than a few weeks. I was always so sporadic with my work. It was always very difficult for me to do something that wasn't creative and stick with it. But now I had to. I had a family to support for the first time in my life, not just me.

We stayed in the red house for the first 3 weeks after Isaac left and I started my new job. Then Beth convinced Isaac to start asking us for rent for $350 a month. The house was paid for and he had to keep the utilities on anyways in order to show the house. Plus even if we paid rent, we would have to leave as soon as they sold it. So the living arrangement would not be a secure one.

That week at work, my co-worker would tell me of an apartment available right beside her and we would end up moving in there right away. My husband would actually build all of our furniture. He built our bed, our couch, our chair, our desk, our end tables. He built everything from scratch. It was amazing. He even upholstered the couch and chair himself.

During this time, Judith was working at the same place which was only minutes away from my workplace. She had to pass our house all the time to go home and yet she hardly visited at all. My husband was just amazed at this. She would tell me that she was going to pick me up after work and always call and make up an excuse to not show.

One time my husband and I went out and stayed with her and Brock. I would never do it again after that time. Brock would ask my husband if he wanted to sit and watch some pornos with him, right while I was sitting there. My husband politely declined and Brock changed the channel. I was terribly embarrassed and just disgusted.

So from then on I would only invite Judith to come and visit us, but that was very rare. My husband saw right through Judith from day one and I think she knew that and could feel that. She always had a hard time looking him in the eyes. She could manipulate anyone, even me. I loved her so much, that I would always want to believe her or trust her.

My husband always saw through her shit. He wouldn't excuse her so quickly like I did. She would do something to mess up or blow me off and it would build up with my husband. He was not a man that pretends. He would be the exact opposite of what I known with family. I was used to a family that covered or hid everything. He wouldn't do that. He would call you out openly.

Our lives together further evolved. My husband became my confidant and my best friend. He would help me see the truth by just being by my side and observing. I never had someone so real.

Judith would never put in the extra effort to see me either. One time she even took her vacation and never told us about it. So just being busy at work wasn't the reason. It was her own choice not to spend time with me. She ended up telling us about her vacation after it was already over.

She was the type of woman that wanted you there in that state or city, but once you were there, you never heard from her. If you did hear from her, she was usually up to something or she wanted you to make some type of public appearance with her.

I always wanted to go visit my grandparents with her, but at the time she just kept making excuses. Finally, I got her to go over there and I brought some dinner to them and I ended up getting terribly sick. It was rather odd. I ended up having to leave early because I got so sick to my stomach.

I've always been very sensitive to people's energy. My body and my spirit have a definite reaction to what I surround myself with. I don't always listen though like I should. Sometimes I force myself to do things because I feel they are appropriate, and visiting my grandparents was something I definitely thought I should do, but my spirit had different intentions.

I would try another time while we were there to go to one of my grandfather's Barber Shop Quartet shows and I ended up getting sick to my stomach at the last minute. I felt so horrible about not attending, but afterwards Judith told me, "It was a good thing you didn't go, I saw your father there." She told me, "He must have been with the group where they take them to go see shows for an outing." What that meant was that my father who is crazy and in a facility (according to Judith) was being taken out to a Barber Shop show as a part of their scheduled outings. I had no idea of the truth, so I believed her.

Again, I always felt like I would just "miss" my real father. Judith knew how much I wanted to know this man and sometimes she would even play upon that. One time we were driving on East 6th Street and she very randomly says to me, "Oh, there he is, Patrick just got on that bus. We'll drive back around to see if you can see him." Well, obviously the guy was gone, the bus was gone. She was just doing that to me. She hadn't seen him for years to my knowledge. How would she even know what the heck the guy looked like? She didn't, but I wanted to believe her.

There was even a time my husband had agreed to go with my grandfather to one of the Barber Shop meetings that they had. At the last minute, my husband became terribly sick to his stomach and even got a fever. For whatever reason, we were not supposed to do certain things. Everyone thought my husband was blowing the poor guy off, but he wasn't. It was just another way of the universe putting up a stop sign.

We were definitely there for a reason though. We were in Erie for a specific reason. The closer the time came for us to leave, the more everything began to come to a close.

One day I was working at the technology park and in walks the man that wrote me a recommendation letter to the school board that helped me get emancipated so that I could go to college. He was a college career counselor named Calvin that worked for a local community action committee. I was so grateful because his letter was so sincere. He recalled my goals and knew of my potential. He was that good at listening and paying attention to my aspirations that he was able to put that into words.

I had never had a chance to thank this man and here he walked in to my office to ask for directions. He was lost and went to the wrong building. I almost broke down into tears when I saw him. I had to shake his hand. The poor guy probably didn't even recognize me because it had been so long. He's asking for directions and I'm shaking his hand and thanking him, telling him, "Do you know how much I have always wanted to thank you? You are one of the reasons I was able to get emancipated to go to college."

I'm sure I had overwhelmed the guy, but at least he knew finally what became of me and how his assistance helped me so much. It was just amazing some of the things that were being brought to me at such precise times. That is how my life has always been. I'm never put into a place or location by mistake. I am always there for a precise reason. Sometimes it is for me, sometimes it is for others, and sometimes both.

Being in Erie for an extended period of time allowed my husband to get a good idea of what roles my family played in my life. I would soon see how distant in reality that they were to me.

After 6 months of working at the technology park, another location was being told to us, and now this was Florida. We kept stumbling upon Amelia Island in Florida. We would start researching this area and plan to move there when my contract was up on June 30th. We would even leave that very night.

My husband never could find work there and I don't believe he was supposed to. If he had, we would have likely stayed in Erie and we weren't meant to be there long. It was always hard for me emotionally to be back there. I would recall so much when we were there. But I had to make peace with this place and peace with myself. I needed this to move forward. I got to part with the house I grew up in. I was able to see Isaac get married and move on as well so I didn't feel like I was abandoning him.

Our relationship with one another would never be the same after he moved in with Beth. There was always something in the way. The only time I could get a good conversation out of him was if he was at work or Beth wasn't around. He had trouble talking to me if she was.

Beth after all was an art teacher, you would think we would have so much to say to one another, both being artists, but we didn't. If she was alone and I would try to strike up conversations about art, she would be very quick with me. I think if anything she "tolerated" me for the sake of Isaac, but she was never quite nice to me at all, behind closed doors.

One of the rare times I was driving with Isaac alone, I told him, "Beth does not like me." He said,

"Beth likes you, why do you say that?" I said, "Because it's true." She didn't want anything to do with me. She would speak more to my husband than me.

We had been there for Christmas and I was so excited about that. I never had a stable income where I could buy my family gifts, but we had a little extra to spend. Not much by all means, but I was proud of the little we had. My husband and I went out and bought Isaac a new pair of boat shoes. He had a pair that was tattered and had holes all on the side where his toes hung out, so we wanted to replace them for him. We bought them a brand new coffee maker to replace the old one that Isaac had for years and brought over from the red house.

We never once saw any of it. They still used the old coffee maker. Isaac never wore his new shoes. We asked about it once and the topic was quickly changed. My husband, I believe, even thought they gave the coffee maker to Beth's daughter, Vanessa.

I thought our little gifts were so sincere. It was these little things that added up. I even recall at Isaac's wedding, the photographer took a picture of Isaac and me together. I always loved that photo, but I would never see it again. All I saw was the proofs and Beth never ordered that one. I believe we had a picture of us in the wedding party, but that was it. All the pictures hanging around their house of their wedding and not one of them had Isaac and me together.

What killed me is he knew me. At least I thought he did. I had loved him terribly and always told him how grateful I was for him in my life, but perhaps he had forgotten those moments.

Being back in Erie was only a reminder of what I had left behind and a reminder of the things I thought I had, but didn't. Acceptance of my own reality was forever upon me.

We would leave behind everything, including belongings. All the furniture my husband had built, some of it couldn't even be removed from the house.

Two girls ironically that I worked with were going to move into their own places and needed furniture, so we gave our bed and our desk to the one and sold our washer and dryer real cheap to the other.

I hated leaving my husband's furniture. I loved every piece so much, but we couldn't afford to store it or move it anywhere. Neither one of us drove. We only had $5000 dollars saved up for our move which wasn't much when you figure about $1500 of that would go to a place to live.

We would head to Atlanta first to visit my husband's mother and brother. We would stay there for a few weeks and then she would drive us to Amelia Island. It would be such a warm welcoming break for the both of us.

Chapter 15

Ameila Island, Florida

We had moved to Ameila Island, Fernandina Beach, Florida in August 2001. We would meet our landlord named Bob which we would soon become friends with. He was an older guy about in his early 60's and just a sweet man. I always called him "Bobbie" and he hated that because it reminded him of his mother calling him, but I always had to say that. It just flew out of my mouth constantly.

We loved it there. We would live right across the street from the ocean. We could hear the waves at night, it was beautiful. The town was quaint and the people were friendly give or take a few. We were happy though and relaxed.

That December, Isaac would contact me to tell me about them driving down to see his sister that lived about two hours away from us. They were going to rent a condo there for about two weeks and then drive back. So they had invited us to come and stay for a little while.

We took them up on the offer and went down there. I have to say, Isaac still at this point tried to put effort into our relationship. He may have altered his life for his wife, but he still had a little desire to try and be involved in my life and marriage. It wasn't much, but I appreciated what he gave.

I ended up feeling as though I came down with the flu while we were there. I felt terrible for a day or so. When we got back to our home in Florida, I would soon find out that my little flu was actually a sign that I was pregnant. I was nervous and scared. I had old fears resurface. I was secretly afraid of my husband abandoning me, but he never did. He stood right by me and supported this beautiful experience we were about to share together.

We were living off the unemployment check I had from my job. We lived off of $1000 a month, $600 for rent and the other $400 was for groceries and miscellaneous things such as internet. Neither one of us had luck with finding work there so we had to make some decisions.

Charity, my mother-in-law, who was so excited about having a grandchild had offered for us to stay with her. She picked us up a week later. All the things we just bought for our new place would be left behind again. Now we only would keep what fit into the SUV that we rented and away we would go.

I cried leaving there. I liked our little place so much. We were going to miss Bob too. We enjoyed his company and friendship. We hung out together, talked, and would cook food for one another. He lived right below us so we were always around one another. But we had to go, my unemployment was going to run out in February so we had to make decisions based on this new life we were about to greet.

We moved in with my mother-in-law and brother-in-law in a 2 bedroom apartment in College Park, GA. After we moved there, I ended up finding out I was able to get an extension on my unemployment due to the current unemployment rate in Pennsylvania. It was an extreme blessing as my husband and I always had a great deal of trouble getting work in Georgia.

All of us were cramped in the apartment. My first six months of pregnancy, we slept on the floor in the middle of their living room. Not long after we arrived there, we kept hearing a puppy out in the woods. I would go for little walks by myself on occasion and I saw this black little puff of fur run into the sewage pipe. Nights had passed and the puppy would just howl such a sad howl.

It was Easter Sunday and drizzling outside. My husband and I would go outside and try to find this puppy. After just hours of my husband chasing the scared dog back and fourth in the woods, he finally took and old white sheet and snuck up on the little guy and caught him. The dog was so worn out, we thought he was dead.

We put him in the bathtub and put warm towels on him and nursed him back to health. We ended up keeping him and calling him Easter. He would be the strangest dog we ever had, but he would be the first introduction to parenthood that we would get.

My mother-in-law realized we all needed more space and was willing to take whatever action was necessary. Three months before I was due to give birth, she closed a deal on a house in Jonesboro, GA. We would move again and now into our own bedroom, a 9x12 square foot room. It was a small room, but it at least gave us a little privacy. We were simply grateful for Charity extending her home to us.

About a few months prior to our first son being born, I was "nesting' and preparing for the arrival. I made a shrine in the corner of our room. I set up a crib (which by the way, we used only twice). I put on the bedding. I adorned the top of the crib with stuffed animals and toys.

I had a special candle set up on a table along with different items I felt would be a gift for our child. I often spent time in front of that shrine at night praying to my creator, our child, and the universe as a whole. Spiritual occurrences would begin to happen after I would go to sleep. Around 3-4:00 o'clock in the morning would be my little ones active time in the belly. (This turned out to also be his active time at night outside my belly.)

My husband would often stay up at these hours working on the computer. Every night around the same time, there was one stuffed animal that would move feet away from the corner of the crib to the center of the crib. My husband would leave the room and then come back to find the stuffed hippo placed perfectly in the center.

So my husband started playing this game with "him" and tried to even trick the little one by almost attaching the tag of the stuffed animal in between the crib guard, and still the hippo was moved into the center of the crib. No matter what my husband did, the hippo would be right back in the middle of the crib every night.

The covers would also move on top of the crib like something was walking on top of them and the crib would creak all on its own. It would only do this during the baby's active times at 3-4AM. The night before his birth, the movements stopped. After he was born the occurrences never happened again.

Another occurrence was that one time my husband was in the kitchen getting something to eat and I was in the living room with my mother-in-law. I had just got done eating some cheese and crackers while I was in the kitchen, but my husband had no idea that I did that. Cheese and crackers was a very common snack for me to have during my first pregnancy.

So I went into the other room and sat down while my husband was in the kitchen. Then he said

"Why don't you come in here and get your own cheese and crackers, you were just in here." I said, "Honey, what are you talking about, I didn't ask you to get me any cheese and crackers." My mother-in-law agreed I hadn't said anything.

Here he heard a little girl's voice say "cheese and crackers." We had no idea whether we were going to have a girl or boy. The thing is you never know what form the child's soul was prior to being earthbound. You could actually give birth to a boy, but then the presence of their soul felt female because of their prior life experiences.

The closer we came to the birth of our child the stronger the occurrences would become. I ended up giving birth on September 12, 2002 to a healthy baby boy we had named Fletcher, at the time, based on the street we lived on in Florida.

We desperately wanted to leave Jonesboro. The energy there was terrible. Our new baby would just be so sensitive to people there that we could hardly go anywhere.

My role as a mother would become my number one priority. I embarked on this journey of parenting along with my husband, as a great privilege. I wanted to do so much. I just fell in love for a second time with becoming a mother. The experience in itself would make me take a very realistic look at my own parental influences.

Some people are born "parents" and some evolve into their role. And some never appreciate the responsibility and the obligation they owe to their offspring. Part of becoming a parent is not just becoming a teacher or friend. It is also about becoming a student, as our children teach us invaluable lessons about ourselves.

During this time, my husband would be enduring a darkness and a battle with an old evil. The same evil that had torn us apart before in our past life was visiting us again, but we had no idea of its meddling. This darkness would almost break us a part.

One day, I had reached my breaking point and was at the point of leaving. My husband had become so consumed with this darkness that he hardly left the room. He wouldn't go anywhere. He was consumed fully by this dark matter.

It was at this point when I broke down crying before him that he awoken into a different state of being. It was the oddest thing I ever witnessed and it would get even odder.

At the last minute, my husband would be summoned by his guides and now he would listen. He spent hours in meditation in the garage, something he rarely did for the time while we were in Jonesboro. He was in a trance like state. My voice and even his son's voice would not jar him out of it. I tell him about these times even now and he hardly can recall being in these meditations.

My husband was always intuitive and sensitive to others energy. So sensitive that he would try to avoid his intuition and even "shut it off" while we were in Jonesboro. We both hated the way we felt there. There were so many old spirits present there that you would see dark bodies all the time. It was just a stagnant place for them, like they never evolved after their passing.

There is no explanation for the multiple levels of life we live. It is even more difficult to explain these levels to someone that cannot see them. So during this venture and awakening, I thought that this was it, that this was the end of our relationship. That my husband would not change and would not see what was going on.

But he fought back. He started listening again, to his guides, to his God. He also needed to remind me that in this life, that darkness would not win. He was visited that night. He fell asleep downstairs on the couch. He had just gotten to sleep when several robed men stood around him. He would be called by his real name for the first time in this life. They would tell him of me. They would tell him of us. They would call us by our names.

He was visited by God, although he could never see the being, it was just an amazing bright light that appeared from behind the robed men. He was told that we needed to reunite ourselves with one another. Now my husband is also a skeptic, an intuitive skeptic at that. So he said to the men, "How do I know what you are saying to me is real?" And they brought before my husband our little boy, and our son said to him, "Please Daddy don't give up."

The next morning, my husband would ask our son, "Did you come to visit Daddy last night?" Our son looked him right in the eyes and said, "Yes." It would be my husband's confirmation that he heard the truth.

My husband would now fight to not give up on me and to not let me give up on him. It was a very emotional time. I thought my world was crumbling before my eyes. I felt abandoned because I could not bring him out of that state of darkness that he was in for so long.

Then it was one night, my husband knelt before me, and he told me of these spiritual visits. He told me that his grandfather was present. He had passed on when my husband was 13. He told me that my grandfather was present and was speaking, but no sound came from his mouth. Then he told me, that the robed men, the guides before God, told him our names. We were finally able to know our names.

My husband said, "And now I am going to tell you our names..." He paused, and then out of nowhere, it was like some force had come and threw him off to the side of the floor. This force was so strong that it had literally thrown his whole body feet away from me. He was knocked out cold. I ran to his side, shook him and even lightly smacked his face. He was completely limp. Minutes later, he came to. He said, "What happened? Did you hit me in the head with something?" I said, "No, you just completely moved and were thrown over to the side of the room." "You were just getting ready to say our names for the first time and then it was like something hit you and knocked you out so you would not say the names."

What was odd too was that my husband hit the floor on his left side, but he said it felt like something hit him in the head on the right side. Something definitely didn't want him to tell me our names.

But my husband knelt before me again and I closed my eyes and he held my hands and said, "Your name is Meilena and my name is Valdormar." As he said our names, chills ran down my arms, and tears ran down my face. I remembered now. As he said our names, I remembered how we spelled them. I remembered our truth. I remembered why we fought so hard together. It wasn't Valdormar that I was angry with it was the energy that tried to keep us from loving one another.

We had always vowed to return to one another, that we would seek each other out, and we did, in this life.

Now we both remembered more of our lives before. In our past life, I always told Valdormar, "If we ever have a son, I want us to name him Mandomere, as that is a very strong name." It would explain to us that that was why we never could call our son by his birth name that we gave him. It too, felt wrong to say. And our son never wanted anyone to call him, "Fletcher." He was only going on two, but still couldn't stand to be called that name.

From that day forward, we would call one another by our names. Finally, we could speak to one another with our real names. We still had pieces missing though. Our last name would be one of those missing pieces. So my husband would listen to his guides and soon he was told our last names and that would be, "Hauslendale."

I had published two books under my previous name and would immediately re-publish them with my new name. I couldn't even bear to be called or referenced by my old name any more. However, I would have to go by this name at my place of employment until we legally had the name changed.

Once I found out my true name, I could go by no other name. It was the fakest feeling I ever felt to even be called that.

We told our son his name was Mandomere Hauslendale and he immediately said the name in its entirety. We only told him it once and he wore it like a glove. He never associated himself with the other name at all. But this name he owned right away.

At last, we knew. Something major in our life was missing and it was our names. How do you explain this to others? This sounds entirely insane, but it was the truth, and sometimes the truth is the hardest thing to convey.

We would immediately sit down soon after and tell Charity, my mother-in-law. She was around us and had witnessed some of the strange occurrences we spoke of, so she knew we weren't just making up some story. After all she never could call me by my old name. Both her and my brother-in-law called me "Little Girl."

Now she would call me Meilena. As for my husband, he never at all liked his name. He never understood why he didn't like his name, but now he knew.

We would soon embark on a journey back to Erie. We needed this change. We needed to get out of Jonesboro. The house where we lived at was very uncomfortable. Before we left a spirit even approached Mandomere, he was only 2.5 years old when this happened. He was in the living room and Valdormar heard him speaking to someone. It was a little old black lady, she asked him how he was and if he wanted a doughnut.

We never gave him doughnuts yet so he didn't even know what those were. The place was undeniably cluttered with energy. That was why we felt so crowded. Day or night spirits were there.

So we packed our stuff up and hopped in an SUV, and moved up to Erie into an apartment Judith would tip us off too. My husband and I were both working now from out of our homes and things were moving for us once again.

The last three years were very lagging. Even moving to Erie gave us a sense of renewal. I wanted to be there so that my family could actually meet our son. We saw Isaac and Beth only twice over the course of those 3 years and they literally only visited for about 4 hours total each time even though they were there for 3 days.

It was very embarrassing for me. Valdormar's family was just completely surprised at how quick they wanted to leave. I would cry every time they left. It was like a slap in the face. It was a courtesy visit. They would travel all that way once a year for 4 ½ hours. It was hard to amuse them to even stay that long.

Judith came to visit once after our son was born and stayed for about a week which I gave her credit for. She even bought gifts for our son and for me which was appreciated. She of course had to throw in some drama though and give me her insurance policy right there in front of everyone and made a big deal out of it. That was embarrassing and unnecessary. And then goes into, "so when I die…" I didn't care about some insurance policy she just changed over to my name. She probably had just did that because she knew she was going to be leaving her husband soon and wanted to get him off of it.

Needless to say, I had enjoyed her visit though. She is always a different character when she is out of her own element.

Erie was calling me though and after those three years we had to go back for something else. I soon would find out exactly what for.

Chapter 16

Revealing the Truth

The trip up to Erie was surprisingly easy. Our son who was terrible making trips in the car was all of a sudden enjoying the ride. Things were working out for us and our family had a renewed sense of togetherness. We needed this after some of the recent occurrences. My mother-in-law would hate to see us go, but she knew we needed this as well.

We would get to our apartment and start being able to buy things for the first time in three years. We had both only recently found work so we were so grateful for being able to just buy furnishings and clothes. We had our own space too and this was important.

I knew before we even arrived that our return to Erie had something to do with Judith. Something wasn't right. I could always feel her no matter what state I was in. She would think she could lie to me being that I wasn't there, but I would call her out when I was sensing otherwise. On two occasions over the past years I would feel her relapse back into alcoholism. Sure enough I would mention it to her and ask her about it and be a day off of her starting drinking again.

In the course of two years, I did this twice. She would then confess when I asked her about it. When we first arrived, she would be the one to give us the keys. Her aura and everything was terrible. I could see it before we even got out of the van. She hadn't seen me for a couple of years and didn't even come up and hug me.

She trembled. Her head just shook. Her hands shook. She could hardly stand up. She had trouble speaking. Her words slurred. It was awful. She looked like a 70 year old woman. It just killed me to see her that way. Every drop of ambition was just gone from her eyes. She couldn't even look at me.

She came over a day or so later and wanted to plant flowers together, but she couldn't even stand. She almost fell over in the front yard. I had no idea how she was even driving by herself. She almost ran over a kid backing out of the driveway. This woman has angels. I don't care what she ever does, somebody watches over her ass because she always just misses danger.

I then started having decent talks with her. I told her the truth. I told her what she looked like. I told her how she appeared. I asked her what medications she was on. I did research on the side effects and drug interactions. I encouraged her to try and ween herself off of some of the medications she didn't necessarily need. They had her on an extreme amount of Lithium. I said to her, "How is this supposed to be helping you? You can't even enjoy your life while you are on it."

She listened to me and she listened to my husband, every week she was getting better, she was becoming more coherent. I was proud of her by all means. Her body tremors were getting better and better. She was actually able to hold Mandomere now and she couldn't before. I saw her almost every day those first two weeks we were there. I told Valdormar that this was the most time I ever have been able to spend with her and how important it was to me.

He had his intuition kick in though and he told me, "I just hope she doesn't do anything to jack this up. Just be careful." Sure enough one day we went to the health food store together. I was having a fun time and then out of the blue I ask her, "So what ever happened between you and Paul?" Paul was a close friend of hers that she met in AA.

She always insisted that I trust this man. I was introduced to him back when I was 13. She immediately took offense when I asked. She told me she didn't want to talk about it. I said ok. Then she proceeded to tell me that he has gotten a little weird. I start asking more questions and then she proceeds to tell me that Paul and her had sexual contact with one another. Well this was no big deal to me, until she told me that their sexual interaction involved me.

Here the picture that I had sent her of me and my son at Christmas time was blown up so that she could make a mask of me and wear it while giving Paul a blow job. She proceeds to tell me how he was always infatuated with me and liked younger girls and asked her to wear a mask of me.

I was literally shocked. I don't know if many more words came out of my mouth. I was blown away. Then she dropped me back off the house and left. I was just shocked. I immediately told my husband and he phoned his Mom.

Here the picture she told me she had blown up for my grandparents was not even for them. It was for her own sick pleasures.

I couldn't even speak to her for about a couple of weeks. At which time, I had found out we were expecting our 2nd child.

I would get a dream the night before we found out we were expecting that I was pregnant. It showed me the baby boy. It also told me that this child would be very different for us. That this child would go everywhere we would take it. With our first son, we were very limited with situations we could expose him to. As a baby he was very sensitive. He didn't like stores. He didn't like baby carriers. He didn't sleep for 6 hours straight until he was 6 months old. Even then, we did third shifts with his sleeping schedule. (Ofcourse his sleeping pattern and store anxiety changed after we left Jonesboro, now you can't get him to leave a store!) He was a definite night owl.

My dream assured me that this new baby would be different. We would soon find out that the dream was right.

We were also living below drug dealers and a prostitute which made for some noisy nights. A day later we had the cops at our door asking if we saw the man across the street move anything. We saw him have two girls over at his house, but only one left. We never saw the other girl again. We did see him sneak out a rolled up carpet. Point being we weren't in a safe area at all.

It just so happened that our landlord came by to pick up the rent and he told us about a one-family house available off of East Lake Road in a much nicer area than where we lived. I was very excited about this. So two weeks later we rented a truck and Isaac, Beth and her daughter helped us move.

We bought brand new furniture as we didn't have anything lavish from before. We brought our stove, and our washer and dryer that we had to buy right when we got there. We even had to buy a refrigerator right away too because the place where we were living didn't have any of that stuff.

So we had to move everything. Then that first night we were there, at 2 AM, we open our door to a whole swat team surrounding the house. Apparently the woman that lived there before us who just moved out was "wanted" and they were tipped off that she was there. We were like, "we just moved in tonight." So then they left.

The day after, my husband was taking a nap on the couch when some crazy looking guy starts to get the key out to open the door. My husband immediately got up and met him at the door. Here this was the girl's boyfriend and he just got out of the penitentiary to come get some of his belongings.

My interactions with Judith were still brief, but she came over here and there to visit. Valdormar was appalled that I would even ever want to see this woman again and now writing it down I can see why. I told her one day though in the driveway, "Have I ever, ever wronged you? Have I ever done anything to disrespect you? If you ever felt that I have say so now." She said, "No, you never have." I told her, " I have always stood by you and supported you no matter what you have ever done to me, but you have crossed a line and disrespected me. I am your daughter you are supposed to defend me, protect me."

I had to go in the house after I was done talking. I felt very faint and didn't need to get myself upset while being pregnant. My husband was just so disgusted.

I was just going through so many sets of emotions. I was enjoying my time with my mother and then she tells me about performing some sexual acts with my picture on a mask. What mother would do such a thing? And then have the audacity to tell me about it? Then act as if it was no big deal and that a simple "sorry" would suffice?

I could feel her brewing though, I could almost see word for word that she was doing something to try and cover her tracks and divert attention. It was like I could hear every word she spoke. I even told my husband, "She is doing something and saying something and I think it has to do with you. She's making up some story."

Sure enough, my intuition was right. She was doing just that. She messaged me online one day and she said she had been trying to send me emails but that my emails must be being intercepted. I told her that I'm the only one that checks my emails so nobody is getting them except for me. She was trying to imply that my husband was intercepting her emails to me.

Only two weeks after us being in our new place, my husband and I both lost our jobs and did not have any unemployment checks to fall back on. We had just spent all of our money on the two moves that we didn't have any funds saved up to prepare for this. Not to mention our employers would make a mistake and send both of our checks to the wrong address which caused a two week delay.

I had $50 left for groceries and that was it. We started scouting for jobs, but had no luck, and we never did with work in Erie. The weather was getting bad out by this time and getting cold. Meanwhile, Judith was plotting. Every day I just felt the tension build and escalate. She was creating her own fury.

Finally, I told Valdormar, I have to call her and put an end to this. I called and she starts saying to me, "I know you can't talk right now cause there are people around you." "We need to be alone just you and me." I was like, "What are you talking about? I can talk just fine. I'll say to you what I want and what I need to regardless of who is around." You could tell she was putting on some ridiculous show in front of someone.

She wasn't even listening to anything I had to say. I started actually raising my voice, but it didn't matter, she would talk over me the whole time. I was trying to tell her that we were going to have to go back to Georgia. She said something to the affect that we were doing this "all because of her." I said, "Don't you get it, we don't have any jobs, we don't have any money, we've got to do something, we have a family."

But nothing I said sunk in. I had gotten myself overly upset for no reason at all. I agreed with myself that I would not speak to her again. It wasn't worth it. I was pregnant and I didn't need the negativity around me.

She was trying to blame my husband the whole time that he wanted to keep me away from my "family." What family was that? We didn't see anyone. And the only time people started parading around outside our house was when Judith started creating this big diversion and panic in everyone. Then all of a sudden different members of her family started calling.

When I had spoke to Judith, she kept trying to get me alone and all I could see was her freaking out and driving me off the pier into the lake. There was a red flag that went off in me. I never out of all these years felt like I did that moment. I was afraid for my own life and my family. She was not mentally well at all. We needed to go and to go soon.

Judith started stalking our house. She would park out in the driveway. She would call her sisters and then have them try calling me. I spoke to no one. I had absolutely enough. I had all that I could take. That was it. She drove around our house and around our neighborhood just trying to find us. We had to be very careful at that time.

The last time I saw Isaac was when I asked him to take me to Aldis to spend our last $50. He just told me he was sorry to hear about our jobs. He didn't ask if we needed anything or if our son needed anything. He didn't ask if we were okay financially or if we had enough food. He just took me to the store for a half hour and that was it. He had to hurry up and get back to a dinner he had scheduled with his Dad and Mom.

I even invited him to come in, my son wanted to see his "Grandpa." Mandomere tried holding his hand, and Isaac just pushed away and said he had to go. My son looked at me and my husband and said, "Grandpa doesn't even want to play with me."

That tore my heart out. I wept right there and my husband just held me. I was back in Erie for a very special reason. We gave these people yet another opportunity to be a part of our lives and they wanted nothing of it.

My mother-in-law was just shocked. Isaac and Beth were the same people that told Charity before she went back to Georgia that if "we needed anything at all, they would help us out," or "they are going to be over our house all the time."

That was hardly the case. Even years ago before, we would have family nights where Beth would cook dinner every Thursday night. Now, they would have the dinners and not invite us or go out and not invite us. I found that out by calling their house on a Thursday and finding out everyone was over there.

Even when I was there, I wasn't there to them. Hardly anyone would speak to me. No one wanted to hear what I had to say. They never asked about my art or about the books I published. They never even read anything I wrote. They would never know who I was or what I aspired to be. The truth was, they didn't care.

I had to come down to the realization that they didn't care. It was a reality that was before me for years, but it was now that I had to look honestly at the people before me.

We were almost out of diapers and we just got our first snow. There was no way for us to get around and we had no money to go out and buy any diapers either. My mother-in-law actually went and Fed-Exed us diapers. That night she went to the Fed-Ex facility, she asked the clerk for the cost to overnight some diapers and it was $46.00. The clerk said, "Is there any other cheaper way you can send these?" Charity said, "No, they need them tomorrow." The lady asked, "Isn't there any family around them that can buy them diapers?" Charity told the clerk, "She has family all around her, but nobody that they can ask for help." So the clerk let her use her own employee discount so she would only be charged $13 instead of the $46, because she knew Charity was doing a good deed. That same night Charity would end up having a small car accident. She was ok, but here she financed a loan on her car for about $1,000 dollars to help come get us and bring us back to Georgia.

I honestly never knew of anyone that would go that length to do anything to help family like she did. She offered us her home again. She had sold the house while we were in Erie and moved into a 2 bedroom duplex, but she offered us her home once again.

There were no strings attached with her sincerity. There were no expectations or deadlines with her offer like there would have been with my family, if I ever were to ask for anything. It was just a real and honest love that family should have for one another. She never through it up in our face either or made us feel bad.

My main concern at this point was to get us out of the craziness before something extreme took place. Judith was very unpredictable. It was time for us to step back and remove our family from her presence. She was a time bomb just waiting to explode.

Charity drove up mid-week and arrived at night. The next night we packed what we could in an SUV and shipped a few toys and off we would go on November 20, 2005.

We had to leave everything once again, but we were walking away with so much more. Valdormar's guide that I always call "GilbertOtis" was communicating with him. I called his guide GilbertOtis because it is like partially his grandfather (Gilbert) and partially his uncle who cared for him as a child (Otis). Gilbert is the sensible man and Otis is the sensible joker, both know what to say to my husband to get his attention.

His guides were telling him, "We are not the ones that failed here." "And Judith was showing us how sick of a person she really is." "You are going to have to leave a lot behind, but that is also part of the example for all to see, that none of what you had in material outweighed what you have in your own family." "You will recover quickly from your losses once you are where you are supposed to be"

The guide was right. We weren't the ones that failed. We were there giving everyone around us a chance to be a part of our lives and to meet our family, but they didn't want to participate. Had they have cared perhaps the outcome might have been different.

Isaac lived under a mile away from us, but we hardly saw him. He would take us to cash our checks or get groceries, but that was it. He came and visited for maybe a half hour or an hour before at our old apartment but that was all. All it would have taken was a little bit of effort, but that effort wasn't there.

I got to see my grandfather one time when my Aunt Peggy brought her girls by with my Grandma. They stayed outside and talked for about 10 before I had to start work. It would be the only time my grandfather would get to meet my son.

We left late at night about 3:30 in the morning. Valdormar made sure we swung by Isaac's house to drop off the tools he had borrowed, as he promised he would return them. Nobody saw us leave and nobody knew when we left either. We were finally headed towards safety. The further away we were from Erie, the better I felt. I was now ready to move on.

Chapter 17

Smyrna, Georgia

fter we returned to Georgia we would now reside in Smyrna instead of Jonesboro. The energy would be slightly better than what we experienced before, however we would still see several spirits along the way. I was now about four months pregnant at this time.

I made one phone call when we got to Georgia and that was it, and that was to Isaac. I needed to speak my mind to him and tell him exactly how I felt. I told him that I was very disappointed in him as a father. I told him that I was disappointed in him as a grandfather.

I told him what our son said the last time he saw his "Grandpa," and I told him how much that had hurt me inside. I told him that seeing me for four hours a year was no way to carry a relationship between a father and daughter. I told him that it was sad that we were only a mile apart and still hardly got to spend time with one another. What was sad was that he wasn't even working at the time and either was Beth.

I told him, if perhaps the reason he didn't spend a lot of time with me and my family was due to his partner, then he could have arranged to spend time with us by himself. He hardly said anything. He said, "I'm sorry you feel that way." He never said anything when we hung up either. No "I love you" or nothing. He would make one attempt to call me and that was on Christmas, but that was it.

Judith somehow got our address and started sending very strange cards. I never read them. I would have Valdormar read them. I was focused more than ever on keeping a positive energy for our little one inside of me. I went and asked the company that let me go if I could apply for another job there, but in a separate department, and thank goodness my old supervisor gave me clearance to come back.

I had to work 3rd shift, but I was willing to do whatever I had to do, to work out of the home. We started saving our money right away and getting what we needed for the new baby as well as our oldest son.

Judith would call our cell phone when she was drunk and leave ridiculous slurred messages. She even began calling and threatening Charity. Eventually we had to get the phone numbers changed.

Holidays passed. Birthdays passed, but I wasn't supposed to have any contact. I was just being innately told this. I worked. I enjoyed my family and in the middle of all the chaos, I published another book.

I thanked God for what I had constantly. I focused on what we had and not what we had to leave behind.

We wanted to make our name change legitimate so we hired a lawyer. This process was the smoothest process we had ever encountered in Georgia. The universe was completely on our side with this one. We even were given a court date of March 8, 2006, my husband's birthday.

We had our court hearing and were granted the name change for our family that very day. It was finally official.

I gave birth to our second son on April 12, 2006. It would be five days before me and my mother-in-law's birthday.

My husband, about a week prior to the birth, would connect with his guides again to find out the name we should give to our child. If it was a boy, we were to name him Hedrick.

We were all so joyous. This was such a beautiful moment for all of us. We were also planning another move that would get our family out of Georgia once and for all, but this time we were bringing along my mother-in-law.

Charity had lived in Georgia for about 10 years. When we moved up to Erie that last time, something just clicked in her. She didn't realize how much she wanted to be around her grandson. When we were in Jonesboro, she had worked constantly and didn't have a lot of free time on her hands. Now that we were back living with her, our lives together would be different.

She was actually coming home after work. She started playing more and having fun. It was a big change. So we searched out a place to live and stumbled upon Fort Collins, Colorado. Charity found a job in her field and applied to it, and they contacted her back.

We would leave for Colorado in July 2006. Before we left once again, we had several spiritual occurrences happen. The first was with Hedrick, our newborn son. Every night I would try to take him into our bedroom after I got him to sleep. He would then wake up crying each time we went in there to lay down. This went on for over a week.

One night, the same thing as usual occurred, so I immediately pick Hedrick up to take him out in the living room, and when I do, I hear Valdormar say, "I caught you, you little shit."

My husband came in the living room and sat down in the chair. He was in a daze, like he was listening to something. He had trouble catching his breath. He had trouble speaking. Finally he told me what happened.

He said, "I kept thinking something must be messing with Hedrick, so I made sure I turned to look this time when Hedrick started crying, and when I did, I saw a little boy run over Hedrick and all of us, then ran into the wall. He knew I saw him and he turned and looked at me and just laughed. He was a little boy about 5 years old, with a thick head of hair. He had a white polo shirt and a blue pair of shorts on." "I asked who it was and immediately a voice came to me and answered, "It's his brother."

Was this to be our third son? We didn't get to have children in our past, so it was not of that time. It was quite daunting. My husband was like, "How do I tell my poor wife who just gave birth to our second son that his brother was picking on him?" So that was a very interesting experience. From that moment on, my husband took a fatherly role and told the little boy at night time that it was time for bed and there was to be no playing around. We never had any trouble from that moment on. We all slept peacefully.

My husband would get taunted one more time, but by a very dark and angry energy. It was only weeks before we were about to leave for Colorado. I watched him while it was happening. He was in the kitchen standing by the stove. You could almost see the goose bumps appear on his arms. He looked around and had a very still look in his eye. I said, "Honey, what's wrong?" Then he told me, a voice said, "YOU DON'T BELONG HERE."

So I told it, "No shit, why do you think we are trying to leave?" We were soon gone and headed to our new home. We had to leave behind some belongings again, but we didn't have that much to begin with. We were ready for the change.

Chapter 18

Fort Collins, Colorado

Our lives were rapidly improving and we were able to have fun together as a family. We always had fun when we were together, but finally being some place that had no prior associations was such a blessing for us. Everyone had a chance to relax.

We didn't have to deal with the traffic of Atlanta and the delays it caused to go anywhere. We didn't have to deal with prejudices of other people towards us. It was a welcoming place and one we would make home for now.

Soon after we arrived in July, I would find out that my grandfather, Judith's father, had passed away on July 17th, 2006. Again I had begun to feel Judith meddling and I was thinking to myself, this is not the time for her to be doing this. Everyone needed to focus on their recent loss, not worrying about me and my family because of some erratic story that Judith was telling them.

So I made a call to my grandparent's house and Peggy and Jeanie were there along with others. I needed to let everyone know I was ok and the reason why I was steering clear from any contact from Judith.

The truth is, I'm a busy mom. I'm a busy wife. I don't have time to focus on someone else's poor life choices. Judith is a 52 year old woman. She does what she wants and when she wants. I have no control over where she chooses to focus her energy. The only thing I have control over is how and where I choose to focus my energy.

I may have always tried to keep in contact with her and always tried to do what I thought a loving daughter should do, but now, it was time to get my hands out of the fire.

I could hear Jeanie in the background saying, "I knew you were alright." My intuition was right. Judith was telling her family stories about why I had no contact with them. She was telling her family during this time that my husband was keeping me away from them and that he had convinced me to change our names.

Peggy kept smoothing everything over and saying, "But don't forget she's your mother…" When was everyone going to stop making excuses for her? People have been making excuses for this woman, all her life.

"That's just the way Judith is." No. That's not just the way Judith is, that's the way Judith chooses to be. There is a difference. If you were born with a physical handicap, I would tell you, "That is just the way that you are," but if you were born normal and progressively chose to handicap yourself and your relationships with other people, then I would tell you, "you made that choice."

Just as I was being told to call my grandmother's house, I was also being told to call another person I had not spoken to for a long time.

On November 20, 2006, I had an intense instruction to call Isaac. It had been almost exactly a year since we had left Erie. His number was flashing in my head though. I hadn't even had the number written down and what was even odder was it was his home phone number. I almost always called their cell phone first.

I was trying to ignore this urge, but then my body just started vibrating and the number kept flashing in my head, so I called right away. I would call their home phone number and Isaac would be there, and be there by himself. The first thing out of Isaac's mouth was, "This is very strange that you called, your father just called me yesterday out of the blue."

It was at that precise moment that I knew why I was meant to call Isaac now. Patrick was trying to find me and neither Isaac nor Judith knew how to get a hold of me.

We spoke for a little bit and I talked to him. I told him that he was actually mimicking his relationship with his father with me. I remember when Isaac was younger and his father lived in Cleveland, OH. He would come in and spend a few hours with him and that was it. Maybe toss $20 in a card for a holiday or a gift certificate to this one restaurant, but that was all. No real content there. And I remember how sad it would make Isaac. He never told me he was sad, but I always sensed a strong disappointment from him towards his father. Now the tables were turned, and here Isaac was presented with the opportunity to correct this behavior through his relationship with me.

Instead, he had done the same thing. When I told him about this, he was like, "I never really thought of it that way." I can only imagine it will be years before he even sees this pattern, if he ever sees.

My phone conversation with Isaac made me do a search for Patrick. I paid for a people search to be conducted and it pulled up his address, so I sent off a Christmas card to him. I never did receive a response.

I continued working at home and writing. I finished my fourth book in February 2007.

I would get another vision that would persuade me to action. One night sometime in February, I awoke at 5:30 in the morning abruptly. I had seen Judith grasping her chest and having pains, but she wouldn't pay attention to them, and kept putting off the fact that she was about to have a heart attack. My dream was telling me that the only person she would listen to about going to the doctor was me.

I awoke just shaking, so I promised my guides that I would call as soon as I awoke, if they would just let me go back to sleep. So when I awoke I had called my grandma to get Judith's phone number. I called her and told her my dream. Here Judith said that all week she was having sporadic chest pains. I told her to get checked out to be safe. I asked her about Patrick and here she had the information I needed, his cell phone number and his address, which was different from the address I had acquired.

So my dream just could have been a way to trigger me to contact Judith to get the information I needed to reach Patrick. It had been over a year since I had spoken to Judith. Here she said she he gotten sober after a drug overdose and stomach pumping back in February 2006.

I was very grateful I was not involved in this episode of her life as I was nearing the birth of our second son, so it was a blessing.

It's not easy to walk away. But there comes a time and point where you have to do what is right for yourself. You have to do what is in the best interest of yourself and your family. As any decisions that I made not only reflected me as a person, but my husband, my sons, my mother-in-law, and even our dog. My life had evolved outside of the people I once knew.

I can't change people. I can love them to death, but in the end I can't make choices for them, and I can't walk for them.

I got off the phone and shortly thereafter called Patrick for the first time in my life. I was so nervous I didn't know what to say. I was shaking in my voice, I could feel it. The moment I had always wanted was now before me.

Months ago when I paid for his address, I was even nervous to tell my husband about it. He accepted the idea open heartedly, but I was living off of old fears. Judith's family had always shunned any idea of contact at all. Even one of Judith's sisters that works at the same hospital facility that Patrick goes to, declared that I wasn't missing out at all on this person being in my life, "His brain is just mush, he did way too many drugs, and now his brain is just mush."

So I had no idea what to expect. The last I knew the guy had to go to the hospital every day. Some people even made it sound like he was living in a mental facility all his life and was just a walking incoherent zombie that may not even have a recollection of having a daughter. I lived with this. I accepted what I was told, but that never stopped me from wondering about him.

In my heart, I always felt he was misunderstood. I actually felt that he was some what of an intuitive man. Sure I could be wrong and I could be delusional, but it was always just what I felt. For all I knew, the possibility did exist that he wasn't my father at all. At the same time there was some intuitional sense he had towards me and I to him for some reason.

So I had no idea what to expect. Could he speak to me? Would he know how to carry a conversation? I mean I was expecting him to be somehow incapacitated from what others were saying, but I also wondered how he obviously was coherent enough to call and ask about me and want to make contact.

I called and he answered right away. I asked for Patrick and there he was. I was now speaking to him. The first thing he said was, "yeah your mom just called me and told me you were going to call." I had internally sighed, like "ugh, the biggest surprise I could give, and someone called and told you about it already?" But he said he was glad she called because he was getting ready to leave to do laundry. I was thinking to myself, "Ok, he is capable of doing laundry, interesting."

The man was hilarious and very intelligent. Judith had told me he was schizophrenic so I didn't know how many people I would be talking to. Would I offend him for calling? Would I trigger some emotions? I had no idea what to expect.

Here was a man who had met his common law wife 7 years ago and has happily been living with her on his own. He wasn't living in a facility. He was coherent of his life. Now yes, he does have a mental history and is diagnosed as paranoid delusional. But, he is "there." I was probably stumbling over my own words more than he was.

I started to feel more at ease part way into the conversation. He said to me right away, "You are the girl I have been praying for every night." I had so many questions that I always wanted to ask but became speechless and dumbfounded.

I told him how I called Isaac a day after he had called him. He told me when he first called Judith she had freaked out on him. I found out about the call through her sister Peggy months prior. She told me that Judith immediately got her phone disconnected. And she told Judith not to send any pictures or give out any information on me. Well, Judith did send him pictures of me. He told me he had them hanging on a bulletin board.

He said that before Judith disconnected her phone, he had tried calling one more time and she had apologized for the way she acted. She said that she didn't take her medication that day. Apparently she is on some other medication that I am unaware of now.

He told me that he bet Judith never told me about David. He said his last name, but I had no idea who this person was. I never heard her mention him before. Apparently she used to get messed up and tell Patrick that David, his best friend, might be the father.

I couldn't help but think to myself how even then Judith got off on putting people in drama. Here David used to give Patrick a ride to work and Judith claimed that they were together intimately and that there was a possibility that he was the father.

This came as a rather big surprise as I was told by Judith that the father could have possibly been Snoopy Slater, a guy that died in a motorcycle accident long ago. Patrick had apparently heard that as well. But everyone always told me, "No, no, Patrick is your father, Patrick is your father." When it came down to it, I guess it didn't matter, regardless of who my father was, they were not there and they weren't present in my life.

I told Patrick my life had been "interesting". He said, "That's putting it mildly." I don't know how much he knew. I got off the phone with him after we talked for a bit and was just surged with a variety of emotions, and then even more confusion. I wanted to ask him for a paternity test. I wanted to somehow put both of our minds to ease, to finally have some undeniable confirmation of the truth without having to have Judith's hand in it at all.

I had called him again the following day. I had a gut wrenching feeling that Judith would be contacting him a lot more. I had to tell him that. That feeling I had was right.

I wrote a letter to him. I wrote everything that I felt, thought, and wanted to ask him. I wanted to know so much. I wanted him to know what I was told. But I also wanted him to know what I believed. My questions would go unanswered.

I called Judith on my 32nd birthday, April 17, 2007. It was then that she told me she stopped by to visit Patrick and drop off some cat food. You don't casually just drop off cat food to your ex-husband's house and visit with him and his companion. My intuition was right. She was calling him and paying him visits.

She told me that he got my letter and was going to have his companion help him write back. Judith also told me that he would be moving. I tried calling him, but he never answered.

I left a message with my phone number when I called again, but he never called, and that was it.

Did Judith say something to him to scare him away? I was just left with this pit in my stomach. I knew she had told Isaac things about me that wasn't true at my grandfather's funeral and he believed her, someone that knew me growing up. What was a man that didn't know me going to think if she placed such thoughts into his head? He had nothing to base my character off of, only our two conversations.

She told people a lie about my name change even after I had told her the truth. I always wanted to be honest with her no matter what it was, but she would not reciprocate that honesty, instead she would use it against me once again.

I did the only thing left for me to do and that was to write this book. This is my truth. This came from me. Will I offend someone for speaking of this truth? Surely, but I can guarantee that the people that know me won't even read this. And for those that do, it would only be to see what I said about them.

Will I ever get to know my father any further? Will I ever get to see or test paternity? I don't know. What I do know is that I started writing this book as a letter to my father, what I discovered, is that I really wrote this book for myself.

Now I can see and reference before me the sequences of my life that have led to this moment. I would not change a thing as each moment had its place in my life for a reason. Each moment was a lesson in time, to allow me to draw upon my strength and my faith.

This book does not denote the end, but the beginning... Onward Rising. I have left behind people in a timeframe of all their own. Sure I still call and check up on my grandmother or some of Judith's sisters, but I will always be "one" person to them, the person they had isolated in a particular timeframe of my life. It is difficult for them to grasp my personal evolution, part of that is due to older age I suppose, and the other part is due to denial.

My accomplishments were always kept "little" no matter how "big" they were. Nothing has changed.

I love what I do and for where such people disregard my efforts, there is always many more that take recognition. My husband being my primary greatness, but also my children, who have allowed me to heal that part of my life that I grew up too quickly to experience.

The pattern stops with me.

It is in life, once we acquire awareness, we cannot return to the way we lived before. We cannot return to the darkness once we have been shown light. For now we know of something more. We know a different path can be before us. Now we know a life of greatness, a life of joy, and a life of love.

Awareness does not make us change our patterns or behaviors right away. We will walk the line between the positive and negative until our conscience decides which role in life that we should keep.

Refuting patterns often means changing our scenery, our social surroundings, and our associations with those who no longer or never had our best interest at heart.

We no longer have to love out of leisure. We can now love out of purpose. As we move forward, we can do so knowing that in our hearts, the love and energy we gave to others, even if unnoticed, had a reason for being present.

Moving Forward… (a year later)

I never did hear from my father again. After that one brief encounter, I received one letter 6 months later, however the return address was not even valid and his phone number had been disconnected. As to why he would contact me after all this time and then want nothing more to do with me, is beyond my words. I can only say that although our encounter had sparked more questions about my life, it also did provide answers.

We choose our paths. We make the decisions on who we involve in our lives and the responsibilities we choose to maintain. I now know that my father despite mental history is able to live a life outside of facilities. He is able to make choices, which is something I did not realize before.

There will always remain in the back of my mind whether or not my mother was faithful to him during their brief marriage, and whether or not I was truly his child in the first place. But regardless, I was connected to him in some way, enough to intuitively keep an eye on him.

___

My intentions for this book, was to write it, and to send my father a copy, but that opportunity did not take place. I see now who the book was truly written for... myself.

Not only is it important to move forward in our lives, but it also important to know just where we came from. Writing this book allowed me the great opportunity to see the events that had taken place in my life in a sequential order. I was forced to remember situations that I may have tucked away for comfort.

I am grateful for the experiences that I have had however bitter sweet they may have been as it has allowed me the ability to write and to convey to others how we can rise above any situation. We can become the better person we were intended to be. Our experiences in life were never intended to lessen us as individuals. Our experiences were intended to be used to make us more of who we are.

www.ingramcontent.com/pod-product-compliance
Lightning Source LLC
Chambersburg PA
CBHW030911090426
42737CB00007B/162